T0130017

CRUMBS AND TREASURES FROM THE BASKET

EAGLE ANNIE

BALBOA.
PRESS
A DIVISION OF HAY HOUSE

Balboa Press books may be ordered through booksellers or by contacting:

Balboa Press
A Division of Hay House
1663 Liberty Drive
Bloomington, IN 47403
www.balboapress.com.au
1 (877) 407-4847

Print information available on the last page.

ISBN: 978-1-5043-0409-2 (sc)
ISBN: 978-1-5043-0410-8 (e)

Balboa Press rev. date: 09/05/2016

INTRODUCTION

Many people have a truly traumatic life: often with horrible, unmentionable things happening. This is especially so when there genuinely seems to be no way out of the pain and suffering.

God never, ever abandons any of His people who have been through such horrendous things which often cannot be talked about. He never abandons them to their own devices, which are only limited to say the very least.

He is constantly with them, watching, caring, loving and supplying their every need. However, if we do not begin to use our minds and hearts in simple faith to investigate and eventually appropriate the precious promises he has for us. The battle can become an endless chase for happiness and well being. We watch dogs sometimes chasing their tails and see that they are never able to catch it till they sit down.

Many people are never set free from their pain, suffering, sin and sense of being permanently lost. But that is never the fault of our heavenly Father. If we are not prepared to genuinely sit still from time to time and surrender the never ending chase for our way of supposed happiness, while still embracing with a stranglehold our pet hatred, unforgiveness or angry way of dealing with issues, then we will miss the hidden treasures available to us.

I have needed to find a way in my personal walk with our loving Father not just to survive but to have an abundance of treasures of high value to share with others. He has blessed me in such a way that often I feel like a spoilt child receiving an extra chocolate frog when no one else knows about it.

Two of the main ways He has brought me to the place of joy shall never lose their power and value.

Firstly He has shown me that there are actually messages of His wonder and splendour in everything everywhere and at all times. To follow suit with this theme He has also so often shown me that there are hidden treasures in every one, everywhere at all times and in every situation.

However, most of the time, it is up to me to sit still with Him and have a good look for them. Not all treasures from God are spiritual either, many, many times they can come in the form of natural gifts, like the smile of a child, a flower that someone hands to you, a beautiful little bird that comes unusually close for no apparent reason. And the list goes on. The natural gifts either wear out or fade away with memory, but the spiritual gifts will remain forever. Still I must say here, even when we see the gifts of blessing and bounty and somehow we find it hard to pick them up, we need to ask ourselves is there some fragment of bitterness or unforgiveness or fear or even a sense of unworthiness stopping us.

As we hang on to the negative things and hold them close to our heart there is no room left within to place the new found treasures.

But be encouraged, God shall never give up on helping us until we have been enabled enough to lose the unnecessary things of life and to make room for necessary things and the treasures of life.

I thank Him for that.

I would like now to share just some of those things which have brought me to a place of gathering, many treasures to begin filling a special box, called my heart.

Many of the treasures are like great pearls to me, because of the way they have been developed with my pain and His precious love covering them to make something beautiful of them.

You may ask, is this all worthwhile in the looking for treasures in our times of pain and deep loss? Yes, oh yes oh yes it definitely is.

You may ask is this a truly scriptural thing to actually look for treasures at all. Again yes, yes, yes it is; for scripture says:

Reference {1}

IN ITS TIME GOD SHALL MAKE
ALL THINGS BEAUTIFUL

But we won't see it unless we look for it.

SPECIAL THANKS

To these who have given very specific and loving
encouragement for the journey of this book.

First and foremost I give thanks to our heavenly Father because it was Him who specifically planted the seed in me to write a book when I was just eight years old. Though it has taken sixty years to get to this point for this specific book, He continually put things into place to develop and prepare me enough to start the journey.

Then to:

MOTHER AURING
PASTOR PHILIP BLANZA
IMELDA AND EDWIN LIWAKEN
DIANNE AND JOHN LINDSEY
AND LAST BUT DEFINATELY NOT LEAST

To my husband Bill for always believing that
writing is the main thing in my life.

CONTENTS

"REAL LONELINESS"

Have you ever been so lonely that you felt physically sick? Well in one way I hope so, because as a Christian we certainly have come to the right place to learn about the only true and safe friendship with daily companionship that will never fade away or betray us in any manner.

When we learn the value of His precious friendship I believe we will never again be lonely as we live by experience His written word with the promise;

Ref {2}

"I shall never leave you or forsake you."

At one of the loneliest times of my life {as a Christian}, I was living in one of the picker's huts on a medium size tobacco farm in the foot hills of a well known mountain. The farmer and his family, which he was very close to, lived on the property, and several workers living on the property also, for it was in the middle of tobacco season. I had gone to bed reasonably relaxed and happy. In the middle of the night I awoke with an acute awareness of being alone and having no one to talk to about the things that mattered to me personally, and certainly no one with which to work through the loneliness hanging around in every fibre of my being. I clearly heard my heavenly Father say into my heart "Get up and go to the door and have a look around"

For once without arguing, I arose almost instantly and went out to the veranda at the front of my hut. It was one of the most beautiful night scenes I had ever seen. The moon was fully out and shining with unusual strength and beauty that particular night.

There was a band of thick, foggy mist floating approximately three feet off the ground, a light frost on the grass sparkling in the moon light and some cows lying asleep scattered here and there around my hut. The atmosphere seemed strangely warm and hard not to enjoy. I so desperately wanted to share what I felt about what was visibly before me. My heart broke again with the acute awareness of being on my own; I broke down and cried almost uncontrollably as I turned around and went back inside. As I walked back into my door way, again my heavenly Father spoke and said "What is wrong with sharing all your treasures with Me. Don't you think I love you enough to understand what you are going through? And don't you think I might feel some of the same pleasure with seeing some of the same beauty as you look upon it?" I was so blessed to hear Him ask me to share my best and my worst times with Him. It has taken many years to really enjoy with deep heart contentment the fact that He would want to share anything at all let alone all my moments of joy and whatever else I may go through.

I have married a good man since that time, but mostly speaking, he enjoys MENS THINGS, like cars etc.

I appreciate what I can share with him, but I appreciate even more the wonderful fact that I can share everything with my Lord and Saviour at all times of the day and night, without him becoming agitated or impatient with my thoughts, words and girly things.

Oh how I praise him for that.

{Ref 3} Hebrews 13:5

"ORCHARD TREASURES"

When I was a toddler of just six years old, we used to live on a very large orange orchard. I spent many hours walking or running through the rows of trees smelling the citrus blossoms and eating many of the sweet fruits that grew later on the trees. Often I would half bury myself in the cool sand and just listen to my father, who would be working down the back of the orchard yodelling at the top of his voice. He had a marvellous voice and his music always reached to all the corners and boundaries of the property.

I was always awake early of a morning waiting till the parents would stir so I could do whatever I had to for the day and then run into the orchard and play again.

I have always believed in God, but didn't have much understanding about Him or what it meant to belong in His family as one of His beloved children.

This particular morning I was thinking again of the beautiful fruit trees waiting for me to enjoy them, and then quite clearly I could hear a strong man's voice say to me

"Get up and go to the wardrobe and take out the string of pearls that are there for you."

I did not know who it was that spoke, but did know it was someone who I was safe with. I knew it was not my natural father's voice and anyway, he was still asleep.

I had no comprehension whatsoever at that time about how pearls were made or the value of them either.

All I did know from that very moment onwards was that I had to see and pick up something beautiful that belonged to me. I arose quickly and looked in the wardrobe across the other side of the room. I was seriously disappointed when I looked in there I saw that it was totally empty.

Not only were there no pearls but also no clothes hung in there either. I got back into bed with a broken heart and wondered who it was that had spoken so clearly to me. I had investigated the room thoroughly to make sure no one was there and looked outside and saw no one was there either.

That was the beginning of a sixty year hunt to find the pearls that I knew belonged to me.

I did not understand for many years that it was indeed my heavenly Father talking to me, but of things to come when I was ready to receive the understand it.

Nor did I recognise that He valued my words given to Him in simple trust, and that in fact these words offered to him in faith were going to become my actual pearls of great worth.

I have come to know since then that words of worship and of faith offered to our heavenly Father are treasured by him. I have come to know that our words spoken in love and with His direction can become like treasures to others. However the hidden treasures of those words or pearls of wisdom are often formed through great pain as He covers them with His spirit, the special substance needed to form their value. Thus they become pearls of great price.

Meanwhile; Nearly every jewellery shop I would come to throughout the following years I would go inside and investigate all the beautiful pearls and ask myself the same question each time; Is this what He was talking about, are these the ones for me.? Occasionally I would feel yes, yes these are the ones but I could never afford to buy such beautiful things, and anyway I believed I was not good enough to own such precious things.

After approximately fifty years of searching for what I thought was to be forever mine. He spoke to me again and told me to start gathering pearls for the work of His kingdom purpose. Then quite suddenly I was accumulating many hundreds of pearls, waiting for further instructions of how to use them. When I had gathered approximately 35 thousand pearls of reasonable quality He showed me to use them to make jewellery and raise funds for the mission fields in the Philippines', specifically for the children; which I did do. Until that point of time I had never had any interest whatsoever in the Philippines' or anything to do with the people of that nation. It wasn't long before I learnt that the "Philippines" are actually called in many nations "The Pearl of the Orient" which thrilled me to the depths of my heart.

As I worked with them, I became more deeply hurt because of a total lack of understanding of the journey I was on. I wondered why I could gather so many precious things and not be allowed to keep them for myself. I became almost obsessed with their value. For to me each pearl had been created through the process of great pain in the darkness of the oyster and I knew not all people valued pearls or respected their journey to come into being just so people could own a rare beauty or wear them around their neck or in some kind of jewellery.

I was deeply saddened at the fact that most people will not even count a pearl of any value unless they meet some particular man made standard. To me personally every pearl that exists is highly valued, and every pearl is a success. After all they exist therefore they are of real value. I handled every pearl that I collected and saw much beauty and worth within them. I became obsessed with anyone being able to handle and respect them, so I began to keep many for myself, until the Lord told me to give them away. I did but it hurt deeply. Often that would include some pearls that I finally saved up for and wore with joy as I highly valued them. Those particular pearls always brought tears to my heart and my eyes when I felt the Lord was saying to the soil of my heart that it needed to be ploughed up thoroughly and prepared for something quite special. This entailed my accepting the fact that God wanted to hear my words and counted them as His personal treasures. I was being prepared to confidently know the value of my own personal words or pearls as I gave them away to others, even if they were unable to see any value in them and discarded them as worthless and lacking beauty. I am a person who would love all people to love pearls and would love to give them as an endless flow. However I am learning who can and who cannot accept them as Father God helps me to know the right time and way to share them, just as He is showing me how to share words. I can now rest in peace and share the fact that I actually have a few rather nice pearls and enjoy wearing them very much as I see my worth in Him more and more. Yes, I am also ready to give them away if ever I feel my heavenly Father is saying to do so; for after all He is my main treasure and not the pearls. Then one day He began to show me what the original conversation was about. The original wardrobe I was to look in was indeed simply a thing of the future. It was a representative of the place where I would put the clothing and things which I used, by choice, to cover myself. Eventually I had to get to the bottom of what I could supply for myself and what others from many different walks of life could give me, as I came to the point of picking up in faith what He was supplying for me. I needed to learn the hard way, though the words of real encouragement from people are so needed I was not to depend on them to cover me or show me my true worth or show me what I was. I could only learn what was best to cover myself with, through many heartbreaking times when I felt I did not receive any of what I thought to be normal for all Christians. I did not see for a long time my heavenly Father was calling me specifically and personally from the moment I was born, to come unto Him and that entirety of what He had waiting for me when I was covered by Gods grace and mercy. He loved me dearly and always tenderly, beyond all human measure, as He always does with all of us. He loves us all equally and without favouritism to any. The more I became aware of that fact the greater the hunger grew simply to hear from Him. God was and still is constantly calling me and indeed each and every one of us to simply come closer to Him and take the time to listen. He actually wants us to hear what He has to say. I wanted to hear Him talk to my heart in any and every way possible. Some of those ways are of course, in the written word of God, in His abundance of creation all around us, in the smile or frown on a person's face, in the touch of a small child's hand, in the tears of pain on any persons face and of course so many other unique ways. But I believe at all times God definitely talks to us and teaches us through ways that we as individuals can relate to in our everyday life. He made us and He alone knows us the best. In fact since that first time He spoke to me about the pearls, I have for many years now, been able to see some kind of a message from Him wherever I look. Though I have studied the word a great deal for many years, I did not have to search His obvious messages out through some fancy way of learning. However, I have always had to stand still and look with faith in my heart and not just look with my natural eyes, but my spiritual eyes as well. Sometimes we can actually look for mans approval, opinion or permission and put it on, by choice, like a close fitting garment, before we step out in faith and see, do and receive what our dear Father is attempting to offer to us personally and quite specifically. The more we learn to see, hear and accept what He is saying the hungrier we will be for more of it, praise Him.

Ref {4}

Scripture says He loves us with a jealous love. Thou shalt not bow down thyself to them, nor serve them, for I the Lord am jealous, visiting the iniquity of the fathers upon the children unto the third and fourth generation of them that hate me. This kind of love is not the evil and destructive kind us humans have towards each other at times. It is rather the kind that is perfect and truly knows what is best for us as His precious children and precious treasures. Because He loves us so dearly, He wants to have us constantly near Him so He can teach, lead and perfect all imperfections within us and our hidden character. He does not want us close by to manipulate, destroy or control in any unsavoury manner. He truly wants all that is good and perfect for us. I can honestly say now, I thank God for every living moment of my life with all that it has held for me, which definitely includes all the good, the bad and the apparent unnoticeable things. I am actually glad for every little and big thing that has ever hurt or destroyed parts of me, some permanently and some have since recovered, praise God. Every moment of my life He has just wanted me to see how much He loves me and how much He wants to pay attention to all that I am and all that I do, think, say and feel. I as all of us have to learn, sometimes when man gives his approval or permission to do or be something, it is only a badly veiled attempt to control or limit us. Though we need to be in humble submission unto one another; that means so we can encourage what is beautiful and what is best for each other. It does not mean we can ever have control over or can manipulate what another has in their life, received as guidance from God direct. But it all takes some time to learn and then have the courage to step out and do it. Now, as a pattern of life, I am constantly on the lookout for the treasures hidden amongst the hard times as well as in the good times. I look for the treasures hidden in the crumbs which I receive, even when I am hungering for the greater meat which strengthens Gods children with activated faith and helps them to mount up and fly like eagles. But to remain with eyes on the ground permanently and the meagre scraps of provision there, we will only ever eat like sparrows and gobble like turkeys and retain a negative attitude.

"WHEN THINGS GO WRONG"

Sometimes when things go wrong for no apparent or good reason, we can become a bit impatient, in fact sometimes visibly anxious and even sometimes quite cranky. Most times in my anxious attempts to get things right or to get things moving again I actually mess things up even further. Sometimes I quietly attempt to put things right, and not knowing what I have done, things seem to mysteriously go right again. I am then greatly relieved and progress with what was originally interrupted; as I begin breathing a sigh of relief and giving thanks to our God. Wouldn't it be wonderful if we could do that more readily when things go wrong in our walk with God and our work for Him? I love the way then, when He takes over and fixes things up, as we rest in Him. Mostly we are not aware of what He has specifically done on our behalf. Things just somehow seem to be going right again.

But what happens after we realise there has been,

"Because of the evidence there has been;

"A SURE TOUCH OF THE MASTERS
HAND ON AND IN OUR LIFE."

Mostly, that touch is so gentle that we can hardly say if at all, where He started and where He finished.

“OH I DONT BELIEVE IN ALL THAT SORT OF STUFF”

I always listen to the tone of voice when I hear someone say such things as the above words; because it always makes me wonder; what has happened to make a person actually run away from things which would normally bring joy and celebration to most people. We all celebrate different things and yes in many different ways too; but when it comes to actual anger or despair; something somewhere has gone wrong.

I have also noticed most of those same types of people have a very hard time talking about or receiving the good things of and from God too.

My prayer for all of those folk is this; that they be set free from all the pain that causes them to physically, mentally or spiritually run away and that they are and always will be able to stand still, look God square in the face so to speak. Then open their hearts and confidently with true sense of safety, receive all that God has for them and wishes to pour out upon them with immeasurable abundance.

"DONT ASK QUESTIONS; WHY?"

A minister told me once;" don't ask so many questions." Why I asked?

"You have to be careful that you don't question yourself out of your faith."

Perhaps he had some logic behind that statement, I don't really know.

Perhaps a better statement would have been," Don't doubt too many things" or something similar to that. But my God has made me with a questioning mind; plus His word says

{Ref 5}

Prove all things; hold fast that which is good.

I ask this, how can we prove things without examining it and asking questions about it.?

Any way there are many questions which provide us with great answers, therefore even greater knowledge follows after I personally ask my lord many specific questions.

An example is this; I had listened to a young man speaking enthusiastically about not taking things into your life to fill the great emptiness in our heart. For, he said it only makes the gap bigger. Puzzled; I asked my Lord why that is so? The answer came immediately; Gods perfect, holy presence is actually repulsed by the imperfect and ugly stench of the things of the world and the presence of evil and sin those things bring into our life. Not all things of or in this world are evil and repulse the purity of God's presence; after all He did make many beautiful and wonderful things for us to enjoy and receive, through them, examples of His wisdom and supply. However, whenever we make something or someone more important than He is in our life, then it becomes an idol and even good things can become a stench to Him under those circumstances. I believe it's our attitude about these things, more than the fact we may actually own some possessions. With all our possessions it would be good to remember ultimately all things belong to Him and we need always to have enough room in our lives and plans to receive the true bounty God offers us daily. Then as we pray, fill us oh Lord with your blessed Holy presence, He will and can, with greater swiftness than the light turning on when we flick the switch into action.

If we need Him to fill us with hope and comfort or whatever else we need, then He needs to have all of our heart and will surrendered unto Him to be able do it. Then oh bless and praise Him, He shall not have to recoil from any part of our inner being.

"REAL FRIENDSHIPS"

True friendships are so worthwhile even though some of them have the elements of roses. Some of the greatest roses, including many with the rarest perfume have some of the hardest and most dangerous thorns which may hurt those who approach without proper care.

Though there may be some thorns which may hurt, beyond them you can touch something really beautiful with a sweetness not soon forgotten.

There is always one who is ready to approach every one of us, regardless to the type of nature we have or the issues we carry. He approaches us with all the care that is needed to avoid all damage or destruction, so we as a flower won't be bruised or broken in any way.

Christ alone in His tender, loving mercy comes at all times closer than a breath away.

{Ref 6}

There are friends who pretend to be friends, but there is a friend that sticks closer than a brother.

So then when He shows us our imperfections and very real faults we need not fear the temporary emotional response deep inside us, because just like it says in the good book in ;

{Ref 7}

Wounds from a friend are better than kisses from an enemy.

He not only shows us our faults but helps us to see how we can deal with them and go beyond it to the beauty and strength which lays hidden under the dust of the problem. Even though we are made for fellowship and friendships; it can be difficult at times for we all have some form of self protection. These can be like thorns on a rose. Even though the rose is one of the most beautiful flowers some of them are guarded by the greatest thorns. Still, if we want fellowship sufficiently, we can step out in faith and it will be picked with great care.

The only rose that will not harm us when we get close to it is The Rose Of Sharon, and what a wonderful Rose and friend He is, especially considering the fact that He only wants to share all that the heavenly Father has told Him.

{Ref 8}

"I HAVE BEEN FRAMED, IT'S A SET UP"

I have heard that expression so many times in movies and so on and heard it used in various other ways as well. I have heard people in real life use it too.

A thing like, it wasn't my fault, or I didn't do it, or someone has got it in for me. Well sometimes those statements are true and sometimes there not.

Oh how I wish more people could see the whole process in reverse, for when the lord says to His beloved children; you are my prized possessions, I will surround my righteous ones with my angels.

{Ref 9}

Or when he says;

{Ref 9} Behold I have engraven thee upon the palms of my hands.

Most of us find that so hard to fully accept with resounding joy don't we? But perhaps we could begin to say from Gods point of view; it is a set up, I didn't do it, I have been framed for we certainly have been. For with His blessed, precious, wonderful love He has framed us and set us up to be free in Him and successful in our journey through life on earth.

"I SHALL LOOK UPWARDS"

Lord, you are as much Lord of my life when I am in a mountain top experience, as when I may be in the pain and lostness of a deep valley experience.

Yet it is not that you say; I shall lower my eyes to the valley floor from whence cometh my help.

I have thought about that a great deal, as I lift my eyes up to the hills; I now see that the hill is a place of victory. It is something that I have conquered in regards to sin and problematic situations with your help. It is from and in that place that your help did come to me.

Each time you have met me at my point of need.

I lift my eyes to look at your glory, thus I lift my eyes upwards and out of all that I am and all that I can do with my own poor and limited strength.

Once more Lord God Almighty, all praise and honour and glory go to you.

{Ref 10}

{Ref 11}, psalm 121:7-8 HE SHALL PRESERVE THY SOUL at all times.

"WHAT MANNER OF LOVE THE FATHER HAS FOR US"

When we are trying to make God's blessing fit our purposes, we can get into all kinds of trouble. But when we try to make our lives fit His purposes, then we can get and indeed do get into all kinds of blessings, and that more abundantly.

For many years I have sought Gods will and favour of wisdom and understanding, in a particular area. This being for my own pleasure, but still wanted Him to be involved. I had the opportunity many times of being able to acquire a particular item or possession which I felt would give me great joy. Each time I did so, yes it was a blessing, but it never ended up being quite right; until one day, the same issue came up and the thing of joy turned out to be perfect and indeed what I needed not just wanted. Meanwhile God allowed me to go through the process, with His love and protection of acquiring this particular possession until I had exhausted all my resources in that particular area. When He stepped in and provided for me in such a special way, I finally knew that even when things are only a want, He can still arrange for me to receive them but also see the need of such surprising blessings, after we allow Him to have His way and do it in His perfect timing.

This means, it will happen and frequently, if I allow Him to take over and be in every part of me and my life as I give Him praise and thanks for all things.

"RENEWAL OF YOUR MIND"

I know that scriptures say;

{Ref 12}

Be ye transformed by the renewal of your mind.

Until recently I have mostly thought that meant spiritual matters only.

However, that is not so. Recently I felt our heavenly Father was repeating several times to my heart; you shall be transformed by the renewal of your mind. But it took several days until I began to see just what He specifically meant in that particular time.

A health factor had been prayerfully brought to his attention, of which He was already aware of and He showed me this.

I had to renew my mind every step of the way, to be able to claim the promise which He was holding out to me.

This in turn literally means there is going to be transformation in my physical being and not just my spiritual self. He shows me almost each day now, that for every step of growth in Him and every step of change in any way, in any part of us, we first need to be renewed in our mind and in Him first.

This has shown me yet one more point of needing to be totally dependent on and in Him.

"BABY BIRDS"

I have always found it difficult to deal with seeing baby birds dead on the ground, either dead because they fell out of the nest or dead from heat exhaustion, or whatever other reason.

Still the thing that gives me comfort at such times is the fact that God knows every sparrow that falls. Well, I am inclined to think and believe that means all birds and animals.

All in all they are all His creatures, and many of them have had watchful parents build the nest and care for them till they are able to care for themselves and fly alone.

I feel so helpless and have such a great sense of loss to see much death in this way. I feel this mostly, because I wasn't there earlier to preserve their life and help them to safety. I have the same sense of loss and helplessness also when I hear about the deaths of so many little children.

My only consolation is that our heavenly father, somehow is still in control and He knows how to gather up their precious souls and take them unto Himself in glory. This happens even when I do not hear about these sad times.

"I DONT LIKE THE HOT WEATHER"

Even though I don't like it I do see good examples for our spiritual and natural life because of it.

At the beginning of every new season in most places you see much evidence of people preparing for the impending changes.

Summer time is no exception; you cans see and smell and often hear the burning off that people do to make ready for safety sake during the fire season which will surely follow. We expect it so we prepare for it, mostly getting rid of rubbish and excess undergrowth on the land and in the surrounding bush. We only get our excess undergrowth because of the bounty of rain and sunshine during the previous seasons.

People do the burning off to keep their properties, peoples and possessions safe from the possible and probable raging out of control fires as the season gets hotter and hotter. So I see this as a good time to go through much pruning and cleaning up for our next spiritual and natural hot season.

It not only makes it possible to have better and more abundant fruit growing in us; But it is safer if we have our abundance of new growth kept in good order so that satan cannot trip us up in the new, hot but successful spiritual season of action against him.

"A LIFE LINE"

FROM THE OCEAN TO THE MOUNTAINS
AND ALL IN BETWEEN
THE THINGS WE HAVE FEARED
AND THE THINGS WE HAVE SEEN

THOUGH AT TIMES WE FELT STRANDED
AND CRUSHED WITHOUT HOPE
OUR LIVES HAVE BEEN TESTED
BUT THERE WAS ALWAYS A ROPE

A DESERT IT SEEMED TIME AFTER TIME
AS THE OCEAN CALLED OUT TO YOU AND ME
COME ON REACH OUT AND PICK UP THE LINE
COME HOME BE HEALED AND BE FREE

Perhaps the rope and the call are the love and the heart of God saying come home, I want to love you and lead you.

"SHADOWS"

Often we place an indoor plant outside for a while to get some more light and warmth from the sunshine and a few drops of rain especially after a dry season. This refreshes them, but if we leave them outside for too long in the heat they can burn and die. With just a little bit of wisdom and asking for help when its needed, we can learn where and when to put these plants outside and how long to leave them there.

There are interesting things to see during their time outside. Firstly as the sun moves around, then so does the shadow around the plant and especially towards evening. If we leave them there overnight sometimes we see snails and slugs have visited overnight and left their tell tale signs of holes and slime in them.

Sometimes the same kind of thing can happen to us as we are lead out into the sunlight with God for the refreshing raindrops of His love after a spiritual dry season. If he says to move back into the shadow of His feathers for further healing, or further instructions for a time, but we persist in our own strength and stand there in the same place stubbornly, we can be invaded by spiritual slugs and have holes chewed or torn away in our growth. It can be in those times when we place or leave extra things around us, to create more shade from the heat. The things we place around ourselves may create a shade but do not give room for gods perfect will. And it is in that shadow where satan has things hidden to use against us and move our minds away from acting and living in faith alone and what God can and will provide.

"NOT JUST WHEEL CHAIRS"

TAKE COMFORT DEAR ONES INTO YOUR HEART
YOUR LOVED ONES ILNESS WILL SURELY DEPART
THOUGH PROMISE IS GIVEN FROM GOD ABOVE
IT WILL BE DONE IN HIS TIME AND WITH HIS LOVE
DONT LET THE WAITING TURN TO DESPAIR
OR YOUR PAIN FILLED WORDS CRY IT'S UNFAIR
THE FATHER IS WATCHING AND JESUS IS TOO
AS THE SPIRIT STRENGTHENS AND LEADS YOU
BONDAGE AND PAIN AND CRYING TOO
WILL BE NO MORE THERE SURROUNDING YOU
AS CHRIST GREETS THEM RUNNING IN
WELCOME MY LOVED ONES SO FREE FROM SIN
NO MORE WHEEL CHASIRS OR DOWN TURNED EYES
THEIR FACES GLOWIUNG AS JESUS CRIES
COME MY BELOVED AND RUN WITH ME
THROUGH MY PARADISE ETERNALLY

"ONE GRAIN OF SAND"

If you held a bucket full of sand in your hand you know you could not possible count every single grain. Yet every grain is as equally, very important to the whole bucket full.

If it were possible to remove every grain, one at a time, as we may think it is of no value, soon enough the bucket would be empty. It is exactly the same with all the mighty blessings and provisions God wants to pour out into you and your life just because He loves you.

So if you were to chuck out one at a time, all the things from His bounty, which because of a lack of understanding or impatience you considered useless and worthless, our supply would soon run empty.

"HOW MUCH"

How much beauty and blessing do we miss out on here on earth because pain, sin, disappointment, anger, unforgiveness or simply misunderstanding and many other reasons blind our eyes of faith and harden our hearts against receiving anything? How little or how much do we expect to see and have in heaven with The Master? Still the heavenly Father does not give up on us. He will chastise, lead, prune, nurture, love, protect and prepare us in every way that is needed to open our eyes to all that he has for us.

I know he has much more waiting for us here on earth and in paradise than we could ever hope for or dream about.

In that time we shall see clearly, enjoy more openly than before and accept all which the creator of all of has prepared for us individually and specifically.

He does not throw a few scraps of bread on the ground and expect us to fight over it like sparrows over cast off seeds. He does not give the strongest ones all the goodies and then expect the rest of us to miss out on getting any at all.

He gives to us milk or meat as and when we are appropriately ready to receive it. He has provision and blessing for each of us in ways that are new every morning, and precious things that shall be ours throughout eternity when He welcomes us into the place He has prepared for us. I do raise Him for that.

"TO BE IN AWE OF GOD IS A GOOD THING"

It's when we begin to take Him for granted, or when we start to be over confident in what we are doing supposedly for His sake, that we begin to slide on pride and into danger.

Strangely enough it is also at that time we begin to lose godly confidence in doing the new and bigger things He is preparing for us. We even at times have the nerve to say,

"Oh dear God I am so sorry but you don't really know what you are doing, you have actually picked the wrong person for the job"

God is most definitely intelligent enough to know who the exact right person to do something is, and as always He will prepare them and provide all they need to start and finish well, the job or ministry set out before them. And again how vitally important it is to be in constant fellowship with him to see the right road to travel on, to hear the right directions and methods that are needed. Let us therefore go forwards further into this New Year, and dare to excel, or go beyond all that we have believed in or done before.

I do praise Him, for I do believe it is possible to be and do more than we have ever dreamed of before.

"TRUSTING"

I see my youngest grandchild, a lovely little girl, run around the house so often like a miniature tornado. Every now and then she will stop and go up to her mother or myself, and confidently, silently, place her often filthy dirty little hand in one of our hands and turn it around and around. I watch her face calm down and she becomes so peaceful. After she has made sure every part of her tiny fingers have been touched by the warmth of our hand, she then runs off again like a screaming little tornado getting up to mischief. I have wondered about this many times. It appears as though she comes to me or my daughter for a touch of security and renewal of her strength. I often wonder, because God says that He has engraved us in the palm's of His hands, are we prepared to drop everything we are doing, as we run around like a storm or tornado, and simply go and place our hands in H)is?

Are we prepared for the time that is needed to let go of all that we strongly hold onto, like stress, pain, worry, or even our needs and so forth, and trustingly place our tired, sometimes dirty hands in His? Are we willing to let go of what we are holding on to and by faith turn our open fingers all around till they have been thoroughly touched by the warmth, cleansing and renewing of strength which comes from His hands and love?

Or are we too afraid to lose control of what we hold dear? It is so safe to empty out the burden we hold on to and allow Him to refresh and renew us in all our needed ways. Then we too can continue on with our journey, even if that means at times we may look like a storm or tornado to others.

The word tells us "see I have engraven you upon the palms of my hands".

{Ref 13} Isaiah 49:16

“SPRING”

When spring finally arrives after cold nights and days when we had been wearing extra warm clothes, tucking ourselves into the warmth of our blankets, often asking our heavenly father to hold us and keep us safe. We ask him to keep us from the coldness of satan’s attacks and our own sinful ways. I mention the coldness because sin is a form of spiritual death and death is cold. In spring there is evidence that new life is bursting out all around us. There are flower buds, new grasses, birds and animals acting more energetic and so forth, and of course more sunshine and warmth.

We expect each spring to be new and different. Now then, do we have the same expectation for new spring seasons in our spiritual lives after each heavy and cold time of challenge and limited growth through the times of pruning? Or are we satisfied to tuck ourselves away in what we can provide for our own human protection and growth: out of THE SON SHINE and in the coldness of doubt, fear and unbelief in His divine word and promises?

"WHEN I AM WEAK THEN HE IS STRONG"

We read in the scriptures of many encouraging things that help us when we are feeling a little low or things seem to be more than we can handle well, let alone put right.

One of the major, God honouring, yet encouraging things for us personally is this:

{Ref 14}

When I am weak in my own strength then I am strong in His strength. That is very true but the time needs to come first that we are humble enough to be able to admit that we are indeed weak. Often, after a particular good time with God, when we have followed what he wants, trusted him and allowed him to be our strength and source of direction, we can often see great results. It is in that time we need to keep our ears open to the softest prompting of His still small voice as he shows us other areas of our walk that have slipped into neutral gear.

One area can sometimes be specific things he wants us to pray about as well as taking real action in some work or help for others. It is quite humbling to have to admit we have dropped our guard a bit and in fact become weaker in something of our private lives. Our minds may even tell us,

"Oh well, after all no one can see what I have neglected or become weak in, so I can still tell myself I am strong in all things." When we admit our neglect or weakness to our heavenly father, then he is more than willing and definitely strong enough to refresh our inner man and helps us to get back on the right track. It is good to remember that it is not only the obvious outward things that we can become weak in, but even more importantly it is the hidden things of our heart that often need his strength to strengthen us and put us right again because we cannot do it for ourselves.

PRAISE GOD.

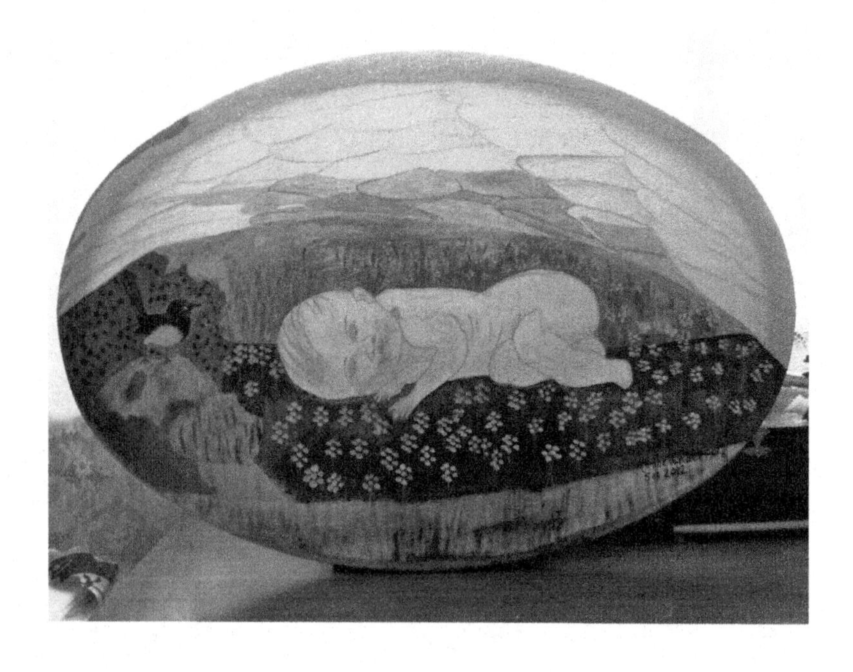

"SLEEPING BABIES"

PRECIOUS BABIES EVERY ONE
DESIGNED BY GOD, UNIQUELY DONE
EACH ONE WITH POTENTIAL RARE
THOUGH MANKIND MAY NOT SEE IT THERE
SENT TO EARTH FROM HEAVEN ABOVE
FOR THE CHANCE FOR PEOPLE TO LOVE
NOT ALL HELD CLOSE BY A TENDER HEART
BUT PUSHED AWAY, MADE TO DEPART
SOME THROWN TO THE GROUND IN DISRESPECT
AND SOME DIED EARLY THROUGH SUCH NEGLECT
DESPISED REJECTED AND UNPROTECTED
BECAUSE THEY UNABLE TO SPEAK,
FOR PAIN AFFECTED.
STILL IT IS GOOD FOR US TO KNOW
EACH ONE IS SEEN WHEN THEY ARE LOW
GODS TENDER CARE AND ANGELS TRUE
WILL ALWAYS BRING THAT DEAR LIFE THROUGH

"IS IT CHASTISEMENT OR ENCOURAGEMENT?"

I suppose it depends on how we view different parts of scripture as to whether we see it as encouragement or chastisement. Often times we read or hear scripture being taught to us and we feel "Oh dear that really makes me squirm and makes me want to run away from it". At other times we feel, " oh boy that is just so encouraging" and then we thank god for it. Here is one of those sections of gods living word which should bless us wherever we are at the time in our walk with the lord. It depends on our attitude and our need at the time we read it. It is exactly what we need to be touched by the holy spirit at all times.

{Ref 15}

Scripture tells us we should be going on from glory to glory. This of course means we are not to be standing still and stagnating, but we should be at least checking out; are we different now than we were a few days ago? Do we think a little more positive according to God's words for us? Do we now speak a little kinder? Do we now reach out in hope and firm belief for others in a clearer and more specific way than before? Are our dreams and goals growing in size as we seek Gods face for all the empowering and resources that we need, or are we sitting on the one spot being prepared to die off in lethargy and self contentment?. Be encouraged,

He, God, has enough faith in us to say,

{Ref 16} "I will be with you at all times. You will complete all that I have called you to be and do, if you allow me to be your true source of all needs'. I have made you strong enough to finish all I have asked you to be and do.

Therefore let us be enthusiastic and share our excitement about going from glory to glory in Him, ALL THE DAYS OF OUR LIVES. I feel to continue on with this theme at this point. I have spoken of going from glory to glory in our daily lives and how we are supposed to walk and grow in faith, actions, words and deeds. Let me encourage you though to remember this, not everything is accomplished over night. Besides that we as human beings cannot be the kind of book keepers as the Holy Spirit is. God does many things we are not even aware of, in His own unique ways of growing us up. Many of the finer details of changes are not even noticed by us at all. Some of those details we may notice but many years down the line as we realise something is quite different now. We often try to figure out exactly how and when the great change took place. More to the point, we try to see what marvellous thing we have done to bring our lives up to the mark of glory God has designed for us to be. Sometimes this can lead to pride "Look what I have accomplished" On the other hand we can become quite discouraged when things in us do not change quickly enough. In those times let us thank God for His marvellous patience and for the fact that He never pushes us into anything we are not fully prepared for. To be able to carry the changes from glory to glory we need a lot of fine tuning and equipping, and He always does it with love and wisdom at a pace we are ready for. Sometimes our rebellion stops the changes which our heavenly father wants for us, but like He says:

{Ref 17} He shall never give up on us. Bless Him for that

{Ref 18} He will never leave you

"SO THEN"

So then, what do we do when we feel we have nothing left to share with people to encourage them to go ahead and grow into all that God has made them to be and do?

Well, we wait upon The Lord and then offer even the tiniest seed and trust Him alone to give it the life and maturity it needs to shine more of His glory throughout the persons face and life.

We also remember that it is not us who can minister the divine revelation to their hearts and cause them to take up what God wants them to have. Prayer always helps us to wait upon The Lord and watch and wait in faith. If all our efforts appear to be failing, perhaps then it is time to wait upon The Lord further and see what He would have us to do.

Do we consider beginning another garden or patch of soil to dig up and wait for The Masters time of rain, then dig it a little more. Then do we begin the planting all over again?

Or do we simply minister directly to God our heavenly Father and trust Him to take care of those we can no longer help and take care of? With all things considered carefully, we need to remember that we are here by His divine appointment and only for His heavenly purpose and not for our own. He is a big God and well able to do all that we desire for others. But we know we cannot do it in human actions that we may feel are needed at times. It is by His spirit that revelation is given to a person's heart and not by human actions. In all the affairs of our heart and in every area of our life; God alone is The Master and the boss.

So let's just praise Him any way.

Amen

"THE SOUNDS OF SILENCE"

When everything is going like a storm in your life, thunder rolling, lightening flashing, people arguing, or even people praising God. When you are asked to do some little or big act of service for God in your local church or for a friend or family member, we may not want to do it.

When we hear bad news of tragic things happening to innocent people, all kinds of crime and suffering all around us, we beg for a peaceful heart and mind.

Oh yes we may give some thanks and rejoice to some small degree. But the bottom line is, if we are honest about life, we wish for the time of total peace and maybe even silence. We may even ask God to speak to us clearly and let us know what is really happening. Often He answers and we hear and obey his clearly given directions. And then joy of all joy, we will eventually hear many good and positive things happening in our life and the lives we care about.

{Ref 19}

BUT what about when everything seemingly goes deathly silent; in those times do we stop still long enough to hear the sound of our own heart beat? Can we still hear the still small voice of Gods Holy Spirit within us? If we cannot, then we have to honestly say "No Lord, I can no longer hear a sound" then that is a good time to trust the one and only one who is still saying

Ref 20} -I shall never leave you or give up on
you; I shall never stop loving you.

[Ref 21} - I shall open my hand and supply all your needs.

{Ref 22} - All my thoughts and ways are higher
than yours. So let go and let God take over.

Just wait till I open your ears again to hear those special whispers I long to share with you, and your eyes of understanding to see the treasures and wonders I wish to show you.

{Ref 20}

{Ref 21}

{Ref 22}

COME ON BOYS - NOT FAR TO GO NOW!!

"COME ON BOYS"

CAN YOU HEAR THE VOICE STILL CALLING
OVER THE MOUNTAINS BOTH NEAR AND FAR
REST A WHILE TO SAVE FROM FALLING
BUT YOU WONDER WHO KNOWS WHERE YOU ARE
YOU ASK YOURSELF THROUGHOUT THE DAY
DID YOU REALLY HEAR IT OR WAS IT A LIE
AND WHY DO THE WORDS SEEM SO FAR AWAY
YOU LOOK AND SEE NO ONE ELSE NEAR BY
SO WHEN YOU REACH THE NEXT HIGH PEAK
YOU LOOK AROUND AND SEE MORE LONELY MEN
AND YOUR HURT AND ANGER ASKS, ARE THEY WEAK
SOON YOU ARE CALM AND CARE FOR THEM
YOU WATCH AND WAIT TO SEE HOW THEY
WILL GO ON AGAIN IN THEIR NEW DAY
EACH ONE LOST IN THEIR SILENT SPACE
UNTIL SOME WORDS LIGHT UP THEIR FACE
COME ON BOYS NOT FAR TO GO NOW
REACH OUT WITH HOPE ILL SHOW YOU HOW
THERES ANOTHER, THE RIVER HES CROSSED
CALLING CLEARLY SO YOU WONT GET LOST
COME ON BOYS NOT FAR TO GO NOW
YOU SIT THERE SHOCKED FOR YOU KNOW
THOSE WORDS WERE YOURS AND SOON WILL BE
COMING FROM OTHERS AS WHEN EACH ARE FREE

"PRESENTS, PRESENTS AND EVEN MORE PRESENTS"

We all love to receive presents, especially when there is no specific reason for it. We are generally in a hurry to unwrap them, especially if we see there has been a lot of attention put into the choosing of the colour of the wrapping, trimming and so on. However, some people do not stop to say thank you, or accept the gift with a grateful heart, and yes even on occasion complain about what the gift looks like, how much they it may or may not have cost the giver. Often we show more appreciation for the gift they give if we think it has cost a lot of money. In our joy and excitement we often go around showing off our special gift, wanting others to see how much someone has though of us.

So then, how excited are we to seek out the never ending special gifts which our heavenly father wants to place in us and in our life? With great excitement as we began to unwrap them and share them with others, to show just how much we are loved by Him and counted as special. Or are we like the people who judge a gift by the wrappings God has on them. You see, God always has and always will wrap His gifts to us in immeasurable love and glory. Do we think they don't look expensive enough to give Him much joy or thanks for them?

The gifts we receive from people are generally to encourage us personally. The very precious gifts God gives us are always meant for the encouraging and the equipping of the body for service and maturity. So the more appreciation we have towards the father for them, and the more we receive them and use them with love, then obviously the more people will know about His love for us and indeed for all of mankind. This definitely includes all the spiritual gifts and the operations of them within church services that are of course when they are led by The Holy Spirit. Or we are going to keep them wrapped up, never opened with joy, never giving thanks to God for them and never showing how much God cares for us and all those around us who need Him and all the gifts He has for them? Or are we going to count them as not expensive or good enough to openly share them with others?

"FANTASTIC CELEBRATIONS"

Many times we have some kind or another of an anniversary to celebrate. Are we celebrating because we can have another party? Are we celebrating because we have managed to stick at the same place or thing for another twelve months? Are we celebrating because we have been able to reach out to the lost and hurting out in the streets and neighbourhood around us? Are we celebrating because we have learnt to repent quicker, forgive quicker and reach out into new areas of faith walking quicker? Are we celebrating because we can now see some areas of needed change in us and our church and we have prayed for answers and God has shown us some strategic plans on how to deal with it?

Or again I ask, are we only celebrating just one more chance for another party and not really celebrating anything spiritually special?

In all that we are and in all that we do, including parties, growth and joyous display of all the fruit of The Spirit we can rely on our blessed Saviour to be with us and provide all that we need. We can rely on Him to love us as we seek out His guidance and direction and throughout the written word, especially our daily supply of living bread.

In fact, He actually promises us that He will prepare a table for us in the midst of our enemies. How awesome is that!

"PSALM 23:5"

{Ref 23}

You prepare a table for me in the midst of mine enemies, you anoint my head with oil, and my cup runneth over.

When we awake every morning, it is a new day.

Every season starts with a new day.

Every year has its new seasons which repeat themselves according to the timing and provisions of our heavenly Father.

We pray with the words of The Lord's prayer

"Give us this day our daily; but do we sit still long enough to ask and then receive what he has got for us in that specific day?

Knowing He alone truly knows every moment of every day what is the best for us?

Or do we assume we already have all we need, simply because we are able to think about it?

It is in those times when we are in a hurry that we are most likely to miss receiving our true needs.

At that same time we will deny God the honour of supplying all our needs as He sees best. If in our time of hustle and bustle, we are also afraid, hurting for whatever reason, in sin or entrapment of any kind from satan and his demon forces, we will often miss out on receiving any of His direction, love and help at all.

Satan makes sure he comes at the most inconvenient time and attempts to catch us off guard.

God alone knows exactly what satan has planned and sent against us, by his powers direct or using other people at times

So by this we see the need of quietly spending time alone with God every day when possible. Certainly we need to spend as much quality time with him to get to know Him and His word better and better all the time in preparation for those times when we are in a hurry.

God's mercies and the table He prepares for us in the midst of our enemies and the midst of our battles are new every day.

So it is good to be resting in that place of His provision, while the enemies are still around, as we are being refreshed with the necessary blessing while being renewed and empowered by His Holy Spirit. Such times are always going to be a time of great celebration. But this will be so only if we celebrate with thanksgiving, and of course doing it all in faith in Him, not faith in what we are or what we can do.

Praise Him, Praise Him, And Praise Him.

"NOW WE STAND SURROUNDED"

BY HIS AMAZING GRACE
BUT CAN WE LOOK UPON HIS SWEET AND HOLY FACE
COME HE SAYS, WE SHALL CONTINUE FORWARDS
BUT THINK NOT UPON GAIN OR EVEN OF REWARDS
{AND HE WOULD SAY}
"HIDDEN AMONGST MY WORDS FOR YOU
ARE TREASURES YOUY HAVE NEVER SEEN
LET NOT THOSE ANXIOUS THINGS YOU DO
BLOCK OFF OR STAND BETWEEN

YOU KNEW YOUR SIN AND SOUGHT MY LOVE
I HEARD YOU FROM MY THRONE ABOVE
AND SWIFTLY SENT YOUR NEEDS BY GRACE
SO WONT YOU NOW LOOK UPON MY FACE?
FOR I SHALL NEVER STOP LOOKING UPON YOURS"

"HIS TOUCH"

A TOUCH OF THE MASTERS HAND ON OURS
WILL DO MORE FOR US IN JUST ONE MOMENT
THAN ALL THE POWER, INTELECT,
TIME, ENERGY AND EFFORTS; OR THE
TOUCH OF ANY OTHER PERSON,
OVER AN ENTIRE LIFE TIME
EVEN WHEN THEY GIVE IN LOVE AND CARE
YES WE NEED PEOPLE AND WHAT
THEY HAVE TO OFFER
BUT WHAT HE GIVES WILL ALWAYS BE PEERFECT
MANS TOUCH AND THEIR OFFERS ARE GREAT
BUT BECAUSE WE ARE AT THIS TIME STILL HUMAN
WE WILL ALWAYS HAVE SOME
KIND OF IMPERFFECTIONS
IN WHAT WE GIVE

"RAIN"

It's raining again and what a glorious thing that is too. We have summer and complain how hot it is.

"Oh Lord, please send us some rain, send anything but just get us out of this exhausting heat"

When we pray for relief, do we really care about what is happening to those around us who might actually need what is happening in the weather and other circumstances of our life? Or are we just concerned about our own personal needs?

We are not condemned to ask God for relief when it is needed, but sometimes it will be an even greater blessing still, if we first give praise and thanksgiving to Him, then ask God what He wants.

{Ref 24}

There is a scripture which says:

If My people which are called by My name, shall humble themselves and pray, I shall hear them and heal their land"

I believe in all things, Gods timing is and always will be perfect. This lovely rain that we have started to get is good for the land, the crops and even our flower gardens.

What a marvellous refreshing they are receiving. It is exactly the same principle in the spiritual realm. Our discomfort is often a part of what God is using to bring greater freedom. Healing and many other blessings to our spirit and all that it needs to fly high like a mighty eagle.

So then if Gods people which are called by His name shall humble themselves and pray not only for their personal needs but for the needs of others as well, God shall hear and heal their land and provide their needs.

This could be a time of being reminded to do business with God for the benefit of others as we help them to take back the things satan has stolen from them.

So, as some would say "Let's take back all the stolen territory" satan has tricked us out of, and deny him the right of hanging around on our God given property and blessings"

It's good to remember too, that rain not only fills our water supplies again but it definitely washes things clean too.

Prayers of love and faith will also help wash away the pain and dirt that satan tries to make cling to another's life.

PRAISE GOD

"FIRE"

By faith we are supposed to stay on fire for The Lord regardless to what is happening around us. We are not supposed to let natural weather and the changing temperatures effect us. But the reality and truth of the matter is that we are often hampered and caused to stumble with the different extremes of weather. In summer it is too hot at times even to breathe properly for some people and our energy level is so much lower, this particular effect includes me.

In winter, especially a truly cold winter, we are all rugged up to try and stay warm.

It is an interesting thing to observe that when many folks are cold because of the temperature they can often slip into a cold mental state, which is a form of depression.

For some it is actually harder to fight depression and sadness and negative thinking in winter than at any other time of the year.

However I know as we learn to lean on the mighty arms of God and learn to actively trust Him to be our warmth, or to be the one to keeps us cool {To keep our temper and attitudes cool} He does, and what a mighty blessing that is too.

However if we are to do things the way God wants, then we all need to be on the alert to see the things the way God wants, then, we all need to be on the alert to see the changes in each other and see what small or big thing we can do to encourage them to go all the way through to whatever victory that is needed at that time.

I believe this is to be real because as scripture says,

{Ref 25} when we even give a glass of water to another in His name, it is the same as giving a glass of water to Jesus Himself.

I think in summer I shall be giving more glasses of water than I have ever given before.

WHAT SHALL YOU DO IN SUMMER FOR OTHERS?
WHAT SHALL YOU DO IN WINTER FOR OTHERS?

{Ref 26}

Whatever you do, do it all in the name of The Lord.

Bless you. PRAISE GOD

{Ref 25} Matthew 10:42

{Ref 26} Matthew 25; 40

{Ref 27}

"STOPPING AND STARTING"

Generally speaking we should set goals and make all the necessary steps to reach that specific point.

Sometimes we start off alright after having sought Gods help and direction and making sure that what we are doing is really from Him and not our own vain imaginations. Our faith is stirred up, plans are set and the journey has begun, then, something happens. For some reason we take a slightly different turn in what we are doing.

{Ref 28}

But, we don't stop to acknowledge God in our ways or check it out with The Holy Spirit to see if we are still on the right track or not. Before too long we begin to slow down, or become just a little grumpy and dissatisfied with things including our brothers and sisters in Christ. From then onwards we are likely to speed up the process assuming we should still reach the goal within a time limit set by us, regardless to the strange twists and turns that are beginning to show up in the road ahead of us. It is definitely hard at times to stop and reset our directions even with The Lords help.

Pride tells us, not to be seen changing as far as our plans and goals are concerned, after all "What if someone thinks we are unstable because of the dramatic way we change things back into order with what God has set out for us."?

I believe I would rather be seen as unstable by mankind but right with God, and then finish my journey safely.

If I am seen as right by man even when I am not and continue in pride, I am likely to get into some spiritual trouble which would be very hard to get out of.

"NO MORE WHEELCHAIRS"

WE WATCH OUR CHILDREN ON THE DANCE FLOOR
SOME IN WHEELCHAIRS WITH OTHERS TO HELP
SOME TRYING HARD TO REMEMBER THE STEPS
SOME BOUNCING AROUND, PLEADING FOR MORE

STILL I HEAR THE MUSIC PLAYED THAT NIGHT
FACES GLOWING AND THEIR EYES SO BRIGHT
THE GIRLS IN WHITE LIKE A PRINCESS BRIDE
AND LOVED ONES WATCHING,
HEARTS FILLED WITH PRIDE

THEN I SEE THAT PICTURE LIFT HIGH ABOVE
TO A PLACE CALLED HEAVEN, FILLED WITH LOVE
WHERE ALL KNOW THE STEPS
AND KEEP PERFECT TIME
NONE NEEDING HELP FROM
THAT WHEELCHAIR LINE
MANY OTHERS HAVE GONE THERE BEFORE
RUSH OVER NOW TO WELCOME THEM HOME
ANGELS JOIN IN WITH GREAT JOY

FOR MORE PEOPLE HAVE LOST ALL THAT STOPS
THOSE BODIES TO ROAM
CRIPPELED BODIES, WHEELCHAIRS AND THE LIKE
HAVE NOW DISSAPPEARED RIGHT OUT OF SIGHT

I wrote this one night at my special needs
granddaughter's graduation ball.

At the same time wishing it could have been the same for
my own first child who is also an autistic princess.

"HAPPY NEW YEAR TO EVERYONE"

May it be filled with new strength, new hope and

"A NEW PASSION."

We all have places we like to go to and things we like to do when we are feeling exhausted and want a little time out. Some sit and have an extra coffee by themselves or with a friend or neighbour as they talk over what has been bothering them.

Some folk ask for prayer or often they forget to ask.

Even though I do not get the chance to do it very often at all, one of my favourite personal places to go for recovery is up in the mountains, alone with God.

Temporarily it's as if my problems are way down below in the valleys. But it is always easier to handle them again once I have had some refreshing time with Him. Even there I have learnt that each time I go up, it is different according to whatever the weariness or problem is about.

I realise, physically going to the top of a mountain is only a short reminder of what joy and victory we can have, even in the valleys as we overcome whatever is needed down below.

The actual journey to the top is always different too. There are always some changes we notice along the way. We notice some varying degrees of change in our reactions to ourselves and in nature, depending where and how we are looking at them each time.

And so it is with each spiritual mountain we conquer. The situation is always different and fresh and God chooses to help us deal with it differently each time. That way He is in control of our constant provision and we learn to trust Him more that is if we allow Him to choose the way for us.

So let us call each day, the beginning of a happy new year filled with His way and His provisions.

"WHAT ARE WE REALLY PREPARED TO DO"

{Ref 29} When the Good Samaritan saw the man who had been bashed and robbed on the side of the road, he did not ignore him. He stopped and dressed his wounds, then took him to a place for the fullness of time that was need for his recovery. Plus he paid all the needed expenses and would have paid more if needed when he returned from his own business affairs. The Good Samaritan was not one of the same tribe as the wounded man. Those who were of his own people wanted nothing to do with him, which included the priests and shepherds and so on.

{Ref 30} We are told to comfort Gods people, those who sit in darkness and are mourning.

We are told {to share others joy}, rejoicing with those who rejoice, and {share each other's grief} weep with those who weep.

When one who is in our church body or neighbour has a friend or family member that dies, do we take the time and effort to SHOW our caring at least asking if how the rest of the family is coping with their loss? Or do we say" oh well I don't know them so it is really none of my business"

Or do we simply walk past and expect someone else to be the Good Samaritan?

I would then have to ask this question;

What if The Lord Jesus Christ himself walked in, in dirty raggedy clothes and sat silently weeping in the back of the church. Then would we care enough and take the time to go to Him and ask if He is alright and what could we do to relieve the pain, and then sit there and weep with Him until He was joyful again, and then have the courage to laugh with Him in His time of joy?

Remembering the whole time as God says in the written word "Whatsoever you do unto the least of these my little ones you do unto me"

Again I ask the question "What would you do and what would you not do?"

When a person is silent, do you have any idea what may be hurting of burdening them, and do you care enough to try and find out or not?

"WHAT NOW LORD?"

Often we ask, "So what now Lord. What do we do now that something has permanently changed in our life? What are we supposed to think, say or do?"

{Ref 31} Well I would suggest that is the perfect time to run for cover under the shade of the Fathers wings just as scripture says.

After all, we are not like God when it comes to knowing everything and how it should all be going.

When the unexpected things happen, it is actually the best time to know God and His ever loving presence and simply let go of the pressing feeling of having to be on top of and in control of everything. After all, only He knows what is literally around the next corner, and what the end result will be to all things that are happening in our life. He wants all things to be working together for our benefit and our good and definitely for His glory.

It is comforting to know, that in all things He knows the end from the beginning, and through it all He will provide all our needs, according to His riches in glory, and according to His own precious written word.

Only He knows exactly all of what's in a person's heart and why they act or react in certain ways. At times those actions and ways will seem to be totally unacceptable to anyone else, and in fact they may be quite hurtful. But, only the blessed Father knows what is really behind all our thoughts, words and actions and yet, He never stops loving us. He never gives up on us and He will never, ever leave us.

So let us let go and let God have the control stick more readily and a lot more consistently whenever things are going well and especially even when things seem to be utterly out of control. That is to say; out of control according to the way we personally expect it to be. It encourages us to know and remember that all things for Gods children work together for our good.

{Ref 32} ROMANS 8; 28

"ARE THEY DISSAPOINTMENTS?"

"OR ARE THEY PREPARATIONS FOR THE PROMISES?"

I firmly believe that God actually talks to us every day and all day, obviously in many different ways. If we could only get used to listening to Him more carefully, from when we first awake early in the morning, we would quickly learn specifically the differences between what His words of promise and comfort are and what our thoughts and desires are.

There are many ways that He lets me know, often early in the morning that I am either going to receive some kind of provision or some words of direction in that day. Words and answers to questions which I have been seeking His guidance on.

If we hang on to these special words of encouragement from H)im and give thanks for them frequently through the day, they can do their work of healing and strengthening in us. So then, when a particular disappointment happens, or something of a real frustration of our plans crops up, we can focus on His blessing that is already on its way and maintain our joy and thanksgiving and not be dragged away to a place of negative talking or even some kind of depression.

If God sees that we actually need some kind of confirmation to what we thought we have heard from him, then He provides that as well.

God tells us to come to Him when we are heavy laden. He also calls us to come to Him when we simply want to share all our cares and concerns, which includes our joys, our sorrows and every other tiny little intimate detail that is a part of our life.

I thank Him dearly that He is well able to care for all of us at all times and without any kind of favouritism. He has always got all the time for us that we need, and we are never too much bother to Him for Him to pay full attention to and look after us perfectly.

{REF 32} If one sparrow falls He knows about that. And are we not worth much more than many sparrows?

"IN TIMES OF GREAT SICKNESS"

We often hear others speak of when they were at their lowest time during an illness, how that the loving Father came alongside in sweet fellowship with them.

Sometimes we may feel joy for them but at other times it really doesn't mean a lot to us personally {if we are honest about it}

But then, when we experience it for ourselves it makes all the other negative times of little rejoicing for others seem so far away.

I have spent a week {mostly in bed} the sickest I can ever remember being. But praise God; yes He came alongside in the sweetest fellowship with such reassurance and deep encouragement.

The treasure of that particular time is this; when the Holy Spirit wants to teach us or simply have some fellowship, it is in that specific time His spirit is talking directly to our spirit.

In those times He overrides whatever battle our mortal bodies are going through. So from that point of view I have been abundantly blessed in a time when normally I could not have even thought straight.

In fact, to try and talk about anything that related to normal everyday situations and conversations was impossible because I could not concentrate long enough to hold a full sentence together properly.

{Ref 33} I guess I am learning to rejoice in all things, just as the scripture tells us to.

{Ref 34} Praise God for all His mercies and great love endures forever, which nothing can ever separate us from.

"UNFAIR"

Let's be honest, how often have we said "It's not fair lord, it's just not fair"? It's not wrong at times to feel that things are out of balance and quite unfair. It's how we handle ourselves and how we respond to what is happening in those times that count. We try to do the right thing by God and by man in attitudes and in actions, but we still see ungodly people around us, seemingly not missing out on any of the good things of life.

If we are not careful we begin to think like scripture says "For they suffer no violence, pain of things that bind them even in their death" Let us be deeply encouraged, God truly does see all and brings to account all people and things that have not conformed to His perfect way. In death those who have led a wicked and selfish life and have never repented or known Jesus as their lord and saviour will know permanent and total bindings of pain, suffering and most importantly, permanent separation from God who is the light and life of all.

Those who live accordingly to Gods way will know freedom, blessing and rewards according to the fullness of His riches in glory when we go to be with Him, because He loves us at all times and wants us to be permanently by His side.

"FEAR"

I have spoken in the past, how fear can stop us from allowing God to search us for all those things which need His divine touch and adjustments. This time it is good to look at another thing that fear stops us from doing.

It definitely stops us from daring to dream and act big.

I know it is right to always wait for clear confirmation before we set out on anything new. Certainly before we say it is from God.

However, we too often say we are unqualified to do this or that. Or we may say "I am not as good as someone else, or I am too much of a sinner and God can use me in such great ways" Qualified people are not always the best people to do Gods special things, especially when their heart is not really open and fully available unto Him and his divine powers and wisdom, trusting what he can do far more than what they can do in their own strength.

When we trust God totally for all skills and abilities to do something and for the supplies to do it with, then we step out in faith and obedience and things go very different. Unbelievable and beautiful miracles can and do happen.

Just let us be sure to give Him all the praise and glory.

How many times do we say to the father "Search me oh Lord and find any bad thing in us and bring it to the surface and deal with it"?

Really we should be asking it of Him every day. But when we do, are we really ready for the soul searching He takes us through?

Because of fear of not being able to handle all that He may show us which is out of order, we begin to run away from Him as He touches on things we want to leave hidden forever.

Perhaps we feel somehow others may see the less than perfect things and reject us. But let us take heart in His perfect love and deep encouragement, because He will only reveal to us what we are ready to deal with. He does all this with perfect love and protection for our soul and whole being.

To be honest it can be a time of great rejoicing and freedom, if we can trust Him and lean on His ever loving arms as He sets us free from all that is less than perfect.

Then He can grow us into the fullness of what is excellent, beautiful and all that which displays His divine nature.

PRAISE HIM.

"CHANGES"

Changes are continually happening in our lives. At times it is hard to keep up to or even understand them.

For instance, when we see that we are coming to the end of winter, we know spring will be following closely and swiftly. Spring always means very real and serious growth all around us. Buds and leaves will be bursting out on the trees and bushes. Bulbs will be breaking through the ground and sometimes where we have forgotten we had planted them.

Grape vines are some of the main things to look at. At this time many growers are checking to see that they are properly pruned of all excess branches, dead wood and twigs, making ready for an abundance of grapes for the new season.

Much care is needed to protect them and make things ready for the possibility of growth as the main branches remain on the vine.

{Ref 35} Without the same care and pruning for us as branches of the vine which is Jesus Christ, we too cannot produce a rich, sweet harvest ready for The Masters use.

But He never prunes more than is needed and we can again take comfort from the fact that He is always working with love and care. PRAISE HIM

{Ref 35}

"WAIT"

Often we are asked by our heavenly Father to wait a while as we trust Him to bring the best things to pass in our lives. However, often we are tired and the battle seems to blind us to His promises and good gifts, so we give up, and usually just before He is about to release what He has got for us.

Like being invited to a grand ball where there are many different courses to the meal.

Balls are usually for specific reasons and the meal is basically the last thing on the list, after many other important activities have been attended to.

Sometimes people get tired of waiting for the desserts to come, so they get up and leave early and the desserts are left on the table as evidence that they left just before the e sweet things are released to them.

So are we willing to wait as long as necessary till the best things God has got for us are given? Or do we leave just before His timing is complete, and before the other important issues {equivalent to meat and vegetables} are dealt with first?

"THINKING"

When we are tucked comfortably in our warm beds, listening to the gentle rain as it falls on our tin roofs, what thoughts come to mind?

Some of the first thoughts which come to mind at such times are about the winds in the forests, rivers filling and flowing with the power of the water which eventually ends up in the majestic oceans.

Oceans rise and fall with such power and the waves roll furiously along. The bottom and the tops of the waves swiftly carry many things along into the shore line during storms.

Some of it is just rubbish, shells, seaweed and many other things which people have thrown into the waters somewhere else. Some of what the waves carry in to the shore can be priceless treasures hidden amongst the sand and seaweed. So I ask, are we used to hearing the voice of our Master Jesus Christ, and what does this make us think of? Do we only ever see the chastisement He sometimes lovingly needs to give us for our benefit? Do we only see the trouble that we and others are going through and blame God for allowing into happen and not for fixing it sooner?

{Ref 36} Or do we at least sometimes think of the wonderful treasures we know that are coming with the sound of His still small voice after the storm becomes quiet again.

{Ref 36} 1 KINGS 19; 12

"LISTENING"

Often when we hear a promise from God regarding the healing for a loved one, we expect it to happen straight away. Plus we hope for or maybe even expect all the symptoms' to totally disappear instantly. So then, I would ask this question "What happens when these things do not happen straight away, exactly as we expect and indeed even after many others have boldly declared, "Oh we know for a certainty God is saying this healing miracle is definitely going to happen straight away?

I am not ashamed to say this, we often need encouragement to wait till the exact time that God has chosen, and not the assumed time man has spoken of so arrogantly.

As a parent this can be quite a devastating time of questioning our faith especially if our child and other loved ones are really going through years of pain and suffering.

We actually question the faith of others at times too.

One thing that definitely helps the waiting time to go better is to begin to believe for the beauty and absolute freedom our loved ones will have as they enter into the kingdom of Christ our king.

He watches over us as does our heavenly Father as the Holy Spirit strengthens and leads us the full length of the road our journey has to go. Just as surely, The Father and the son watch over our suffering loved ones at the same time, and yes, He strengthens and leads them on their individual and specific path just as much and just as clearly as those who are not particularly suffering.

Whatever pain, sickness or bondage our children and loved ones may have during their time here on earth, will soon enough totally disappear. The darkness of sickness and pain will be washed away as the glory of God's presence surrounds them in paradise and show up all that awaits for them there.

The bottom line is this;

God has promised it; and therefore it will definitely happen.

"WHAT ARE WE LEANING ON WHEN ALL ELSE FAILS?"

Sometimes it really does seem as though everyone and everything has failed us.

Not that people have not tried to assist us in some way, and it's not as if we haven't done our very best to do the right thing by God and by mankind as well.

However, there are times there seems to be no answers clearly coming to us, we feel that we have no energy left to fight the good fight of faith. There are times when the weather itself seems to be cold, dark and gloomy with no light or warmth shining upon us.

During those times, until we get back on top of the situation and consciously standing in victory again it seem s as though nothing is making sense and nothing appears to be going right.

Oh I do believe it is those times especially when our Heavenly Father is saying "Lean not on your own understanding"

Even those words can seem to be harsh on our bruised natural minds at times. That is until we start to sing in our heart

{Ref 37} "I am leaning on the everlasting arms"

Notice it says; "EVERLASTING Arms"

What amazing great comfort it is to know, when all else fails, His loving and protective arms are always going to be there ready for us to run into, where He continues to tell us how much He loves us and that He will never give up on us; I surely praise Him for that.

{Ref 37} Deuteronomy 33; 2

"HIDDEN VALUE AND TREASURE"

Scripture says "God provides all our needs" I actually do believe that too. I am however constantly amazed at the many different ways that He does that.

I am also amazed and delighted at the many different ways He speaks to us. Recently I was seeking Him to show me some way I could show something of the value God sees in each and every individual person. I was drawn to the thousands of maple leaves that had recently dropped from the nearby trees. Thousands upon thousands had been blown around by the machine the caretaker of the caravan park where I was staying was using. He eventually amassed a huge pile not far from where I sat on a park bench.

The wind had been playing with them and scattering them in all different directions and he wanted to tidy up the place. I suggested to a lone man walking past that he look at the pile of leaves and imagine they all had a specific number and that one of them had his number on it. Then I asked him if he was able to distinguish which leaf he was or did he think they were all the same, just waiting to be burnt or used for compost on the garden. He could not see any difference in the many leaves. I then told him, that to me as a person he has great value, and to God he had even greater value and in fact he was uniquely different as one made of pure gold, hidden from sight and understanding of all mankind.

Sometimes we can fell just like a withered old leaf of no value, and not even enough strength to hang on the tree any longer. But to God we are all individually and specifically of great value like purified gold, and He knows exactly where we all are at all times. He knows it though we may be going through a time of feeling like dried up, dead, hidden or even lost amongst many others which all appear to be exactly the same.

No one is so lost or hidden that the all seeing eyes of God cannot find them and see their great value.

I PRAISE HIM FOR THAT.

"TO ME LORD"

TO ME LORD
YOU ARE MY PERSONAL PRINCE OF PEACE
NOT JUST EVERYONE ELSES GENERAL SAVIOUR
YOU STAND BY ME BOTH DAY AND NIGHT
YOU COVER ME WITH YOUR GRACE AND MIGHT

IN TENDERNESS YOU CALL TO ME
COME MY CHILD LETS TALK A WHILE
NOT ALL BIG THINGS, SOME BREVITY
BUT SOON YOUR HEART BEGINS TO SMILE

OH JESUS DEAR, THEN LET US GO
MY HEART IS WILLING I WONT SAY NO
FOR IN YOUR ARMS OF LOVING CARE
WELL MOUNT UP AS ONE AND SOAR UP THERE

"JUST A CLOSER WALK WITH THEE LORD"

"JUST A CLOSER WALK'

There are times when we truly ask God to draw us even closer to Him than we have ever been before. We cry and plead all day long and occasionally do some prayer and fasting to make sure we are really hearing from our heavenly father, and to break any strong holds that we see in our life.

But do we really want to walk so close to Him that there is no room for sin or sorrow left between Him and us?

Do we really want to change our opinions or ways of life that may be interfering with our actions of obedience and faith?

He tells us in the written word "Be not afraid neither Let not your heart be troubled. Be anxious for nothing.

Remember I am with you always, even until the end of time. Nothing can separate you from the love of God.

And of course there are many, many other wonderfully encouraging scriptures with promises that we can lean on, and as we do so absorb much strength from Him to be and do all that He asks.

But are we ready to let Him take away all the old way which is far less perfect, to make room for all the new and more perfect way.

It would be good to remember here that His word also says, His thoughts and ways are not our ways, but that they are higher than ours.

He knows the many thoughts He has towards us and that they are all for our good and not for our harm.

The last scripture is one of the main things that are constantly drawing us closer and closer to Him.

All that He has for us will only ever be good for us. But we need to actually ask for them for this activates our faith and stirs Gods activated love and provision for and towards us.

{Ref 38} JOHN 14; 1

{Ref 39} PHILIPPIANS 4; 6

{Ref 40} MATTHEW 28; 20

{Ref 41} ROMANS 8; 31-39

{Ref 42} ISAIAH 55; 8

I praise and thank Him for all of that.

"THE CROSS"

HE WAS HELD TO THE CROSS
BY MORE THAN ONE CRUEL NAIL
HE GAVE HIS EVERY BREATH
AND ALL HIS BLOOD
HE DID IT ALL FOR A PRICE THAT COULD NEVER FAIL
HE KNEW GREAT PAIN
AS IN THE GROUND, HE WAS PLACED WITH A THUD

MY SIN, MY SIN IT WAS THAT HELD HIM THERE
AND I STRUGGLE AT TIMES TO SHOW HIM I CARE
MY LORD COMPLETED IT ONCE AND FOR ALL
JUST SO THAT WE COULD COME
ATTHE SOUND OF HIS SWEET CALL

"OUR BRIDE GROOM AWAITS"

HE SITS THERE NOW
ENTHRONED BY THE FATHERS SIDE
AWAITING THE TIME OF HIS BEAUTIFUL BRIDE
SPOTLESS SHE WILL BE AND
EMBROIDERED WITH GOLD
OH I BELIEVE THIS, FOR IN HIS WORD IT'S TOLD

WHEN WE ARE FREE FROM SIN AND FROM PAIN
IN GLORY WITH HIM FOREVER WELL REIGN
BUT ON THE WAY LET US REJOICE AND GIVE A HAND
TO BRING OTHERS ALONG WITH US
TO BE UNITED IN THAT SAME GLORIOUS BAND.
IT WAS MORE THAN THREE NAILS
THAT HELD HIM THERE
WHICH IS NOW FOREVER FOLLOWED BY
HIS TENDER LOVING CARE
IT WAS ALSO HIS PRECIOUS LOVE FOR US
THAT WE SO OFTEN FORGET ABOUT

"LETTING GO"

As Christians, I believe we all want to learn how to step out in faith and fly like eagles. We make every possible effort doing what we believe God is calling us to do.

Yet more often than not we don't seem to be moving off the one spot.

We certainly don't seem to be flying like eagles on wings of faith.

Perhaps it is in those times we need to see what we are holding on to of our own self effort. I am not against us putting in all the effort that is needed to be a diligent worker and learner of Gods ways.

Stepping out in faith sometimes means the opposite of what we have been prepared for.

It also sometimes means letting go of what we have laid up in reserves because we study, work hard and gather the necessary equipment for. God will always honour our honest efforts to grow:

But, there are many times when God is calling us to step out in what I call raw faith.

In those times we are to let go of all self effort and ability to gather supposed needs to do his work, and depend entirely on what He says to do and what He supplies as we need it.

This kind of stepping out in faith takes real courage and at times can be quite scary.

Instantly satan tries to put us off by such statements as

"You can't do that, you are untrained, unequipped and unskilled."

But when you do step out in these particular times, the rewards are:

Sweet and full of grace and His glory.

{Ref 43} He never leaves us or gives up on us

{Ref 44} AND ALWAYS SUPPLIES OUR NEEDS;
especially when we let Him by getting our limited
knowledge and abilities out of the way of the flow of
His Holy Spirit and His glorious abundance.

Bless Him.

{Ref 43} HEBREWS 13; 5 {Ref 44} PHILIPPIANS 4; 19

"WINTER"

We always have the four different seasons in the weather through ought the year.

Of course each year when we are coming out of the end of a season, how do we know it?

We know it from the simple yet continuous changes that cannot be denied.

The weather begins to be a little bit warmer, there are blossoms starting to appear on the trees and bushes.

In time most of them will bear edible fruit that we can enjoy eating in great abundance; that is if we bother to pick and gather them. Otherwise they will stay on the trees and bushes rotting till they eventually fall to the ground.

Oh what an ugly waste that would be.

But we all do it and much too often too.

We may sit on a veranda for a few minutes or even hours and soak up the sun before we go about doing what needs to be done for the day.

But at the same time we need to be very careful not to allow ourselves to linger too long in that time of doing nothing.

This reminds us that we need to consider carefully that we need to finish our preparation for each and every new season that is right around the corner.

With the warmer weather there are also storms coming and we need to be sure there are no items in our yards that can be picked up and thrown around in the stormy weather which often accompanies the beautiful changes.

There are always many things to look at carefully and consider carefully with all the changes in our spiritual lives as well.

God gives us the signs that changes are coming, but do we sit too long in the soft comfort of our present season and not prepare for the possible storms which often come with the change?

Do we get rid of all possible loose or negative things in us so that satan cannot throw them around and damage us and others; and therefore blind us to all that our sovereign God wants to bring into us and our lives.

This means especially the things that He wants us to participate in to bring about those changes, giftings, provisions and special personal blessings.

Oh yes there is much change coming and marvellous miracles, signs and wonders.

But have we whole heartedly and fully prepared for them, or are we still taking it easy and not really preparing for any real change at all.

"SAYING GOOD BYE AND MEANING IT"

Even as Christians we often come to a very real place of having to say good bye to people, places and even sometimes things. If we face the fact that God is definitely, truly in control of all things, then we also need to face and accept the fact that most of the goodbyes we have to face are actually things our heavenly Father is asking us to deal with and say good bye to as we release them to him. In those times whether we see it straight away or not, He is waiting to place something so special, a treasure, deep into our hearts. When He asks or gives us the choice to say good bye to something or someone, it means He is not forcing us to release something unto Him.

He never asks us to release anything just to see us suffer and be deprived of something we love and greatly value.

It is always to give us something of greater value than that which we have released.

Again as Christians, what we are asked to say good bye to is often in our human emotions. What God is about to place in its place is mostly speaking from the heavenly realms and is spiritual.

Often something natural needs to be removed to make room for the spiritual things, or it will interfere with the actual receiving and understanding of the heavenly treasure and we will never see its value.

An eagle needs to say goodbye to the comfort of all the soft feathers of the nest before it will even attempt to fly by itself.

{Ref 45} Scripture says that we are to provoke one another unto love and good works and honourable deeds.

An eagle is provoked to the good work and freedom of incredible flights while soaring above the mountains and through the valleys looking for food.

This happens as the parent eagles pull out all the soft feathers of the nest and starts to remove some of the sticks around which the actual structure of the nest is made. Only then, because of the discomfort will the young begin to move around more abundantly.

Finally the parent eagles actually push the young out of the nest and make it fall or fly.

The parent eagles, just like our heavenly Father are always there to come under the fledgling and then lift up the wings and take the young to safety. Then they repeat the process over and over again until the young begins to fly in its own strength.

So let us be prepared to say good bye to all that the Holy Spirit brings clearly to our mind and places before us {ref 46}.

At the releasing we shall come to know greater treasures and we shall soar high, as on wings of an eagle. PRAISE HIM.

{Ref 46}

{Ref 45} Hebrews 10; 24

{Ref 46}

"ABOUT MY DEAR MAGPIE"

While sitting on the front veranda one day just watching the rain, a young magpie came up and stood close by me.

I assumed it may have been hungry, so quietly went inside and got some bread for it to eat. I had been over the last few previous years feeding other magpies and thought perhaps it was one of their young ones.

The little one ate hungrily, but then just stood there watching me, with its feathers all puffed up and standing on one foot.

After a short time two other older magpies came up on to the veranda as well. They too ate some of the bread crumbs that were left over.

What impressed me the most about this beautiful display of nature right at my feet was how the young one called out as the older ones came closer.

I at first assumed that was so they could feed it some more of the bread crumbs left there. But the older birds only stood close by me watching and didn't even attempt to feed it.

After a short time the little one quietened down. It wasn't long before the older ones flew away again.

Still the little one stood there watching me for quite a long time, and indeed was still there when we all went inside for the night. It was then that I could see that it was hurting on one side. I wanted to pick it up to see if I could help it in any way, but it would not allow me to.

However I was not totally surprised though, because after all I was a stranger to it.

On the same hand I was really blessed to see that it was comfortable enough to stay so close for so long.

I was also quite concerned to see that its feathers had been totally soaked by the heavy down pour of rain we had just had.

This makes me think seriously how many people around us are damaged in some way, and hungry for food and the loving attention they need to be able to go beyond where they are at.

How many of them are damaged by the storms of life and need time to recover.

Then, how many of them need a safe place just so they can be around other people without having to perform or prove themselves in any way.

How many people like this do we come across which are crying out for some help or support.

There are many times when we cannot understand the cry of another, but are we at least prepared to stop and try to see if we can help or not? I could not help the young magpie, but I certainly could pray and ask our heavenly father to protect and help it till it was able to continue to look after itself.

Again, the next morning I went outside to see if it was still around and if it was alright. It had rained heavily again through the night, so I was concerned that it may not have been able to go somewhere safe out of the cold wind and the water.I was delighted to see that it was still out there waiting for me. Its feathers were all dry now and it was able to move around quite well. This time the parents ate as well while it stood by. Then they all flew away together.

However over the next few days they all flew back again and I was broken hearted to see that there were sores growing all over both of its feet and face and body. Each morning it woke me up with its beautiful song sitting on one of the pot plants right near me.

Each morning for several days its song was a little better and louder. It ate on the first few days but then would come not to eat but just to sing to me till the day it died across the other side of the road. After a few days it could no longer fly so it simply hobbled around in the long grass as the parent birds flew around for a while.

The biggest blessing to me from all of this was the fact that one of god's creatures, during its time of hurting, felt safe enough to be around me till it was no longer able to cross the road to my veranda. It literally gave me the privilege of hearing its last song and indeed I believe I was the privileged one to hear the very best of all of its songs as it gave me personally its best during its time of dying.

I pray I become even more sensitive around hurting people and am able to offer them a safe place of support till they are able to continue on with the rest of their journey.

At the same time I realise that I will not be able to do that without the help of God as he helps me receive my own healing for my own journey first.

{Ref 47} Only then can I pass on or share with others that which has first been given to me.{Ref 47} Ephesians 4:

"COMPETITIONS"

I believe we all like to win whenever we enter any kind of competition.

Many people say we should not gamble in actions or in attitudes.

However, what about the competing spirit we often have even in church circumstances?

These times are usually all done with the words at the beginning "Oh I am only trying to do my best for "The Lord". Sometimes that is quite true and sometimes it is only a religious face we show others, to show them where they are less important than we are. Sometimes it is to show what we feel we are personally good at and others have less value than us because their efforts are different to ours. Therefore we can consciously or unconsciously judge others not to be as good {or so we may think}

During our display of works and human effort are we able to hear the fine and beautiful whispers of the Holy Spirit as he says "Come my beloved and see what I have to show you, simply because I love you and want to bless you abundantly"? Or are we allowing our pride, struggles or even a sense of unworthiness to be in competition with the call of our beloved King and Father.

If that kind of struggle is ever going on, guess what, we are never going to win the competition. And yes, there will be no rewards for our efforts of those times either. Still, because of the patience our heavenly Father has and his love and mercy for each of us at all times, He will never give up on us and all that it takes to get us back on the right track with love and humility towards others. I surely praise Him for that too.

"MISSING THE SMALLER BLESSINGS"

We can often miss many tiny pieces of information which when looked at in the right light and attitude can become as miniature or sometimes even large treasures.

Just as it is so when standing alone on the sea shore, that is till we look down.

"TINY FRAGILE SHELL"
OH LOOK THERE NOW YOU PERFECT SHELL
FROM WHAT FAR LANDS HAVE YOU JUST COME?
AND WHAT GREAT WAVES WITH A MIGHTY SWELL
BRING YOU HERE NOW YOUR JOURNEY DONE?

THE TASTE OF SALT STILL ON MY LIPS
AS I LOOK OUT BEYOND THIS SHORE
THE WAVES HAVE CRASHED WITH THEIR WHITE TIPS
NOW THEYLL NOT ROLL AND DRIVE YOU MORE

"NO HOLE TOO DEEP"

Many years ago when I had youth, better health and greater fitness on my side, my first husband and I dropped the children off at school and decided to go fishing and hunting for the day. We packed our gear in the car and set off to a nearby town where we knew there would be an abundance of rabbits for the stew pot and plenty of fish for the fry pan.

I had begun to build a fernery at the side of the house and thought this would be a good time to look for some wild ferns to collect for it.

We found a comfortable place to do some fishing first and I then decided to take a long walk around the area to enjoy nature and to see what I could find.

It wasn't long before I came to an area that looked promising for what I felt I needed.

I looked over what appeared to be an embankment to a very shallow creek bed and saw exactly what I wanted, many different beautiful ferns lining both sides of the banks. Steadily I stepped down into it and realised it was quite a bit deeper than it looked from the top of the embankment. Still taking no heed to possible danger, I decided to gather some of the ferns that would have looked great in my new fernery.

After a lengthy but an unknown period of time I felt it would be best to gather my ferns together and climb out of that place and go see what game my husband had managed to gather.

I carefully placed the ferns on the gravel at the top of the embankment which I could barely reach, and attempted to climb out.

Every time I placed my foot on the sides of what I thought was a creek bed, it quickly crumbled and caved in even further. I spotted a very large dead tree directly above where I was standing and grabbed at some of the large root system to try and pull myself out, that too crumbled into small pieces of fibre.

I spotted what I thought was a pretty and harmless vine at the side of me. That turned out to be a black berry vine which fell apart after it made some serious scratches all over my arms and legs. Whatever I tried fell to pieces and fear began to grip my heart as all my physical and mental energy swiftly ebbed away.

I began to scream out to my husband for help and he did not come, or so I thought.

I suddenly realised that I knew what it was like to be lost somewhere in the dense bush and could have died there without ever being found, because no one knew where I had gone.

I began to pass out with fear and exhaustion, and then suddenly something lifted me out of there and stood me safely on the embankment above where I had struggled by myself to get out of.

I then walked over to the place where my husband had been fishing and saw that he was quite agitated and concerned.

It wasn't long before I realised it wasn't him who had lifted me out of there, and there were no other people around either.

He had felt that something was wrong and went looking for me. He had walked right past the area of the creek where I had descended into and he heard and saw nothing. I took him to show him where I had been and we both realised that my screams for help should have been heard loudly and clearly.

A short time later we went back to see what the general area looked like and to work out why I could not be heard from the track which ran alongside the creek. Within a few short months the whole area had been totally covered by beautiful, thick lush growth. We never revisited it after that. I found out some time later that what I had gotten into was in fact an old abandoned gold mine which had become unsafe for anyone to work in any longer.

I know I was taken out of there by an angel or by Christ Himself; because it was obvious that I couldn't have climbed out of there on my own and also just as obvious that there were no other humans around to offer me some assistance.

I also know, in natural and definitely spiritual things, there are going to be many times we can become deeply involved in, many things we are interested in without seeing any danger in it. We may linger in those places for too long a time and then find out; by ourselves we cannot climb back up to freedom. Some people may have some general idea what we are doing and where we have been struggling to climb to freedom.

But as they attempt to help us, it's as if we become even more hidden and beyond all human reach to assist us in recovery and freedom.

But this much I know for an absolute certainty;

No hole is too deep or too hidden for our sovereign Lord to find us and lift us out of there.

It is quite noteworthy here to remember, often we receive all the help we need to get back to safety, after we have seen the danger of our situation and after we have utterly exhausted all our efforts and attempts to do it all ourselves in our limited abilities.

I believe it is not only a matter of surrendering everything and every situation unto our Father, especially when we are in danger;

But the greater the danger or need is the greater we shall see the precious treasure of his loving help and protection as he does for us what no one else can.

Bless Him.

"ENDURANCE AND STABILITY"

MAY YOU ALWAYS KNOW
THE WONDERFUL STRENGTH OF
ESTABLISHED BRANCHES
AS THE BUDS OF EACH NEW SEASON BEGIN TO SHOW

MAY YOU ALWAYS KNOW
THE GRACE AND SUBTLETY
OF A WILLOW IN THE MIDDLE OF A FLOWING RIVER
WITHOUT BEING RIPPED OUT
WITH EACH NEW STORM
MAY YOU ALWAYS KNOW THE STABILITY
AND SECURITY AS A BRANCH ON THE VINE OF LIFE
AND WHAT IT IS LIKE
TO BELONG THERE IN HIM FOREVER

"WISDOM OR FEAR"

Is it wisdom or is it fear
That stops our hands from reaching
To touch another or to hold them
And have our tears run with theirs
For how can we encourage their strength?
If not through live interaction
For eyes, hearts and souls have died
But now they strive to live again.
Beyond Those walls they have built so high
Built only because
Of the great pain which has crushed them so.
As they timidly try to drive out fears
While thoughts race and crowd their mind.
How much pain must folk bear alone?
Before we see it in their eyes
So touch them, take their hand and walk
Help them know they can still break through.

"SONG BIRD"

Oh my beautiful song bird
I watch you now as you begin to be warmed.
As you timidly stand shaking your white feathers
And you move to see if it is true
You are still alive; you still exist.
I know the many times past
When you have tried to leave your cage
You flew with such excitement then came the pain
such unbearable pain and the door was blocked
You looked, but still you didn't see it was blocked.
You did not know the darkness was real
You did not perceive the reality and strength of evil
As it prowled about your door
So when you flew to the door your wings were broken
Your heart bled and you almost died.
You trembled with such fear and coldness
Never knowing how to close the door
To stop the darkness from entering in
Finally you went to the back of your cage
You stopped moving
You began to shrink
And still all was dark
Then one day a small light was at your door
A sweet perfume warm and tender

Came drifting gently to your heart
Movement started in your cold heart
Finally light touched your mind
And your ears had heard that distant call

"COME MY BELOVED"

Now light shows your real world
In all its splendour
The mountains to fly over and rest upon
The oceans crashing but after lifting sheets of glory
For all to see, to become a part of and enjoy
All the tiny things too, birds butterfly's and the like
All these are for you to know
You are now a part of the same life that formed them
So now be free, fly with ceaseless energy
Only return to this cage to share with me
All your knowledge and treasures
But don't be blocked again.

"REFRESHING TIME"

Sweet willows green and oh so graceful
Both side are dressed of this river fine
It's cool here now and yes quite peaceful
So each heart is blessed when they give you time.
I see for you the day has just begun
So fresh hope and strength for every life
And thus no pain from the heat of sun
That causes you fatigue or crushing strife.
Now I'll begin again and go on
For my heart and mind will soon be employed
To write and see that good thoughts remain
Just to make sure for others, more life is enjoyed.

"MOUNT VISION"

Many times I have made similar journeys
And yet, each time it is somehow still brand new
I stand at the base of a massive mountain
Its loftiness towering over me like a guardian
Its peak out of sight, as it breaks through the clouds
And they kiss heavens doorways.
As I begin to make my steep climb upwards
The rugged dryness begins to wear me down.
Suddenly I notice an eagles nest
I strive onwards
For I know that, that vantage point is almost at the top
Finally I arrive and clutch the twigs of the nest
for there is nothing else to grasp a hold of.
Only then do I realise how massive my mountain is.
Dare I, an insignificant being challenge such a giant.
Finally I reach the top and look outwards.
The rough road and thirst all behind me now
My heart breaks with joy as I behold the splendour,
For then I am over looking many other great mountains
And lush rain forests
As patches of mist gently obscure
The view of some of the deeper valleys below.
Which way should I go from there?
Should I fly off the top and go?

To the deepest forest full of vibrant life,
Or should I simply soar across to another fabulous peak?

Then I see a tiny, far off road and know
That that is where my journey is to continue
So again I set off not knowing
Where my journey will finish,
Or what it may produce.
Half way down I stop, for I hear
A powerful roar and fear fills my heart,
But then I see a mighty water fall.
Seeming to burst from the very heart of the mountain,
As it cascades downwards, forcing white foam outwards
And I know, there is no fear for this water.
Silently, I watch in awe
As it leaps forward from the greatest heights,
And it does so without hesitation.
This encourages me
And stirs new strength
As its songs of joy and freedom, fill the air and flow through me.
It has certainty of direction;
I don't;
So, reluctantly I follow,
Though with faltering footsteps,
For I am still afraid of speeding.
Finally our journey concludes
Right In the middle of a lush rain forest.
A canopy of pines and oaks, arching overhead,
While sunbeams softly filtered through the branches.
Tall tree ferns standing guard over the finer ferns
And you can see many giant fronds, just beginning to uncurl.
Mosses dress the nearby ground in a carpet green,
While fine creepers' drape themselves
Over fallen tree trunks.

And now I know with deep assurance
That the climb was so worthwhile,
To conquer the mountain
And then make the descent to this haven of rest.
Peace reigns supreme here,
Both for man and nature alike.
Soon I shall explore other mountains,
But for now, all attention is centred in
Just the one, the small bird
Silently hopping past my foot.

"CUCKOO CLOCKS"

All of us have some kind of a clock in our houses; mostly speaking it is simply to keep a track of time, to be able to make sure we get all the things done which we need to in any one day. We have appointments from time to time and would be missing out on many important things if we were not on time.

Many people collect clocks because they like their sounds and their looks.

Folk collect clocks for many different reasons.

One of the styles many collect, are the beautiful cuckoo clocks, amongst them are many different styles and looks and sounds.

But the true cuckoo clocks are all hand carved from special wood from the black forest in Germany. The men who carve them are all master artists and some are actually known throughout the world for their fine works.

Although cuckoo clocks generally speaking are collector's items, not all folk like them or would own one. It is interesting to relate some of the steps of the making of a cuckoo clock to the making of our character as a Christian. The trees for the cuckoo clocks are grown in dense forests and are chosen by people who have a good eye and understanding of the appropriate wood that is needed.

God sees from birth our potential and quality available for his masterpiece, but also sees there are times when we are going to be seemingly lost amongst the rest of the dense forest of peoples and cares. The trees for the clocks are carefully trimmed and prepared for the many cuts and carving to shape the masterpiece. It takes a long time and it doesn't stop until he has brought out the very best grain and pattern He has personally chosen.

Then there are all the fittings of the inner workings and cogs and springs to be put into place. Then there is the tiny door to be fitted so the little cuckoo can come out and give his greeting sound.

These and many other elements of the clock making, cause the price to be quite high sometimes and makes it difficult for many people to own one.

And so it is the same for the master artist, God, to make of us, the valuable collector's item he wants to have with Him in eternal glory.

"DO WE HAVE THE COURAGE TO BE TOTALLY HONEST?"

Sometimes when we are not feeling particularly enthusiastic about our roles as Christian and our specific ministry we may well ask at times "Is it worth while continuing on in the same old path way"?

Well I can say by faith YES, YES, YES it is well worth while, but we cannot do it by ourselves.

{Ref 48} When we feel we have run out of everything of our strength and ability to go any further, and what we have to give to others that is the greatest time to lean on the everlasting arms of God. That is the time to trust Him to take us on to the next part of our journey and on to the next person where we can give something of Him, in his strength and by His blessed, pure spirit.

I believe that is also the time when He will bring to our memory, any and all scripture necessary to encourage us, that is to say if we have previously spent real time reading and studying The Word of God. Sometimes He will even speak some specific thing into our heart just for us alone.

But most of all, I believe he will always be encouraging us to remember that He has never given up on us, that He will never stop loving us, and that He will never leave us. And just to make sure we get the message into our hearts and not just our head, He will continually show us in many different ways that we are precious to

Him and necessary to His overall plan and purpose for this world and His kingdom.

For all this I truly praise and thank Him. And the greatest joy of it all is this;

He has that exact same love and treasure attitude towards us all equally

{Ref 48}

"THE LITTLE THINGS TRULY COUNT"

{Ref 49}

And He will reply to them solemnly, I declare to you, in so far as you failed to do it for the least of these, you failed to do it for me.

When we offer a simple glass of water to anyone in the name of Jesus, it is the same as doing it to Him personally. But when we deny a simple glass of water to one in need we are actually also denying it to The Lord Himself

During the natural season of summer and its hot temperatures it can also be a season of spiritual hot weather with its equivalent hard struggles for many people. Many of us have become dry and thirsty, just waiting for a small drop of cool water or a comforting word of encouragement to help us on our way.

Yes there are many times we do receive our needs direct from God Himself, especially when we hunger and thirst after Him with all our heart and mind and strength.

He is so willing to quench our thirst and many times He will do that through others through what He first gave them to pass on.

We should not allow satan to lie to us and cripple our actions of helping to cool someone else's battle, with a drop or even a full glass of the living water. He, satan, would have us believe we are unable to break the spiritual drought many are going through, but because Christ dwells in us, then we have rivers of living water flowing out from us, not just a few drops trickling here and there.

Sometimes we just need a little help to turn the tap back on Again.

{Ref 50} Mathew 25:45

"I CAN GO NO FURTHER"

Sometimes we are broken into many pieces, scattered all over the ground and seemingly unable to be put back together again, with the appearance of absolutely no value for the present or the future.

Have you ever felt this way? I have and many times too.

But my heart cries for you. Oh my, what a marvellous way to be found by our loving Father.

After all He is the potter and we are but the clay and there are some times when we need to be taken apart, cleaned out and put back together again with a touch of the masters hand of love. But when he starts the job, He always finishes it. Then when we are presented to the world and to the heavenly realm, it is something of great and rare beauty. It becomes something of true value and has many Godly uses.

But it is best seen and best used when it is led by and empowered by his holy spirit.

So in future times when we are tempted to feel and say,"

I can go no further; I am too broken to be of any use to God almighty and His Kingdom service. I cannot see any real advantage of continuing on with what I am doing for Him. I am too tired to even bother trying."

In those times it is good for us to remember in our times of weakness,

It's when God is able to take over in all His powerful, perfect and loving strength and do what we cannot do. Its then that His glory can and will come through in God glorifying miracles, signs and wonders.

So once more, give thanks in all things including the times of being broken.

He cares and will see us through to the very end of time.

After all didn't He promise He shall never leave us or give up on us and He will never stop loving us?

PRAISE HIM, PRAISE HIM, PRAISE HIM

"TO BE IN AWE OF GOD IS A GOOD THING"

It's when we begin to take Him for granted, or when we start to be over confident in what we are doing, supposedly for his sake, that we begin to slide on pride, into danger. Strangely enough, it is also at that time that we begin to lose godly confidence in doing the new and bigger things He is preparing us for.

At times we even have the nerve to say "Oh dear God, you know how humble we are, please don't put me into such a position of such great importance, send someone better that me." It is in those times that we are actually saying "Oh dear God I am so sorry but you don't really know what you are doing, you have actually picked the wrong person for the job." We need to remember God is intelligent enough to know who the exact right person to do something is. As He always does, He will prepare them well for the job or ministry set out before them and provide all they need to start and finish it well.

Again how vitally important it is to be in constant fellowship to be able to see the right road to travel on and to hear the right directions and methods that are needed. Let us therefore go forwards further into the New Year, or new season or the new part of our journey with Him, and dare to excel or go beyond all that we have previously done before. I do praise Him, for I do believe it is possible to be and do more than we have ever dreamed of as we stand in awe of his power, majesty and mighty love.

"FAITH"

Generally speaking we all say we believe what God says in His written word, but do we believe it enough to act upon it and celebrate with thanksgiving before it all comes to pass.

{Ref 50} We are to be calling things that are not yet in existence, as though they are already in existence.

We can act upon and carry that much further than we ever dreamed of; Now to Him who is able by the action of His power that is at work within us, is able to carry out His purpose and to do super abundantly, far above all that we dare to ask or think, infinitely beyond our highest prayers, desires, thoughts, hopes or dreams.

What an awesome promise that is. And just to think, all we need to have is faith as a grain of mustard seed and believe.

Giving thanks in difficult even painful situations is always a part of the preparation to receive the promise of answered prayer.

Once we have prayed and recognise we have actually made contact with God, then we should let go of the asking and continue in prayers of thanksgiving till the answer or provision becomes visible from the spiritual realm into the natural realm. I believe a part of the preparation for all that, is recognising our need of God Himself being more important, that what He can give us or do for us.

{Ref 50} ROMANS 4; 17

{Ref 51}: EPHISIANS 3; 20 {Amplified bible}

"WE OFTEN THINK IN THIS MANNER"

"Oh dear Lord is it really necessary that you continually take us by surprise and allow such unusual and sometimes strange things to happen and take us off guard. Oh Lord it is sometimes hard to maintain a good attitude as you take us through all the new things that you see fit to do.?"

But then I guess if we are always aware of exactly what is happening we may want to change the whole thing to have it done our way.

Then that would be taking all the Glory and control out of the Father's hands.

We would slowly become proud and not willing to surrender our will and what is happening around us, to the power and sovereignty of God Almighty.

After all, He alone really does know what is best for us and for those people and situations around us.

We don't know what's best for us only because our knowledge and power to solve issues is limited.

His power and knowledge is never ending, infinite and perfect in every way and detail; and it always will be.

We see in the written word that He never changes.

One of the main reasons God does much without allowing us to be in control is because we would not be leaning on or depending on Him and the power of His Holy Spirit or even His supportive love and provision.

"WHAT DOES GOD WANT OF US AND FOR US?"

"WHAT DO WE REALLY WANT FROM GOD?"

God wants our heart, reaching out in passionate dependence on Him at all times in all seasons and for all our needs.

He has chosen us to be His beloved, precious children. He desires us to grow into full adulthood, into the fullness of Jesus Christ, day by day and more completely into His image.

He knows we are capable of walking in the fullness of His power after we have accepted His Holy Spirit and begin to obey in the greater ways of faith.

Some of those ways being; praying for people to be healed, raising people from the dead and setting people free from all the cruel and wicked, evil bondages of satan.

He desires actions of obedience for us all to be seen and known as over comers in Him.

He promises us we will be seated with Him in heavenly places.

He desires, but will never force, us to be in constant, close, humble fellowship with Him as the king of kings and Lord of Lords.

He desires us to be aware of all that we have at our disposal for all our needs to be met.

He desires us to be aware of the fact that He surrounds His righteous ones with angels working on our behalf and ministering to us at all times.

He desires for us to know and have a small sample of something of the glory of what awaits for us in glory with Him.

But do we really desire all of that from and with Him?

Or are we prepared to settle for the minimum of second best in life and deny Him the honour to give us all that He has got waiting for us?

"HIS CHANGE FOR US"

What a marvellous fact to think about in Gods promises; He does provide for all manner of things that we need.

We have gone through a scorching summer over many years with many months of extreme heat, fires, many frustrations and many other smaller issues which accompany the season of summer.

However when we can wake up on the last day of summer and see that there is a cool breeze blowing and playing with the curtains of any room, then we are instantly thankful for the change.

There is such a refreshing in that day and the lightness in the curtains as they dance on the air and as they seem to be saying; "Come on get up and let's go play as we chase the birds, leaves and insects as they try to get out of the breeze."

God is gracious with the way He treats us and takes us through all the necessary changes in preparation for each and every new season of our lives.

Still we need to be alert to the smaller things He lets us know about before major changes; that way we can be even more ready when things become different to what they used to be.

When we get too used to things remaining the same way all the time, we begin to take life, God, our neighbours and friends for granted.

But then God steps in and creates the differences that we need to be able to pay more attention to Him as we learn to lean on Him and face the fact that it is He who is in control. We then learn to believe in Him and His word in a far greater way.

As we think further on the theme of receiving much rain to fill the cracks in the grounds of our homes and the dryness of our gardens, we come to see our need of the latter rain also that is needed to heal the deep dryness in our inner spiritual self. There is even more benefit which may be not seen straight away from our rainy seasons.

In the love and mercy which our heavenly Father showers on us through our times of healing and cleansing, He always sees more of what we really are than we shall be able throughout our entire life time.

He knows how much we can take at any one time as He weeds out those deeply hidden things in us that are interfering with our walk and growth in Him.

Just like the flooding rains wash out all the hidden insects, frogs and whatever else lays hidden in the cracks, erosion and so on, so it is with the water of life Jesus Christ within us.

We often need the same manner of soaking up large amounts of Him before the hidden things in us are able to be dislodged from their long time hiding places and are brought to the top.

He never tries to force us to dig in places of our heart that He hasn't first dug out the spiritual and emotional weeds, and done some work to loosen the good soil of our heart that He originally gave us. He alone knows the fullest extent of damage we have done to ourselves or that others have done to us, as we allowed for many different reasons our heart to harden.

The wonderful thing about all this is; He never gives up on us and never leaves the empty spots vacant where something has to be taken out.

I find that the deeper the cutting or pain has been, it is to that exact same level He plants something of great beauty and great value.

He is the great husbandman and knows exactly when, where and how to weed the garden of our heart. Then He shows us what can be planted in there which will grow much precious, sweet fruit for our benefit and the benefit of many others.

He always gives so much of the goodness of His blessed supply and His own spirit to fill up all the empty spots within us.

To do this though, it is necessary for us to spend time, faith and serious commitment with Him and his word, trusting him to bring the necessary and specific words to life within us.

If we do not spend that valuable time doing so, then even more rubbish than before will come back and fill the gaps in us with worse problems than we had before, in fact the bible says seven times worse.

"IN NEED OF REFRESHING"

We look around us at times with thanksgiving for the rain we have. We give thanks to God our Father for the refreshing it gives us and the fact that we don't have to water our gardens for a couple of days or longer.

We also give thanks for the fact that the weather is cooler. Like it or not some of us cannot handle the hotter weather very well at all. In fact we even start in our minds to prepare for the cooler weather we know is definitely on the way. We see signs of autumn; by the way some leaves are already beginning to fall.

Soon enough if we get heavy rain and really colder weather, we begin to speak and complain of how cold it is. As humans sometimes we are never satisfied. But in this entire range of seasons have we remembered or even noticed what has really been happening in the land of our hearts. Summer, in many years, has brought with it long, hot dry days.

The ground in many places becomes so dry and many deep cracks appear. In those places nothing can grow because the seeds have nothing to hold on to. As soon as the rain starts pouring down in a heavy and consistent manner for a while, the ground literally begins to breathe better, it swells up with the moisture and soon enough we see the cracks begin to heal and close over, just like a long standing wound does as it heals. Our souls at times can become dry and cracked open with the heat of the long, hard battle. Just the same as the rain heals the dry ground, the living water will repair and heal our cracked and dried up wounds; that is as long as we are prepared to place ourselves under the healing waters of Christ long enough and consistently enough to give all the time that is needed for Him to complete the job He wants to do in us.

"ON THE SPOT REFRESHING; IF WE BELIEVE FOR IT"

We are often busy doing the things we need to do, fulfilling what the Lord wants us to do in our days of service in and for Him.

Sometimes we are simply enjoying the day catching up on some things we need to know more about.

We become very industrious and deeply involved in study, research and so on.

Then the end of the day has arrived before we realise we have run out of time.

We start rubbing our eyes and realising we are a bit more tired than we were at the beginning of the day.

Suddenly we also remember that there are still a few things to do before we settle down for the night, and certainly before we go to bed to get the refreshing that we need. But let us pause for a moment; "What are we missing here?"

Isn't it possible we can rest in the Lord and wait till He restores our need and energy level to finish the day well and still have praise and thanksgiving moving in our hearts? It really does only take a few brief moments of trust and faith, waiting on God, to be able to continue to finish some of the things we have left to do in the day, but with refreshed energy. It is good to push through and break through the low level of energy at times; but it is even better and quicker when our sovereign Lord and Master does the job for us. Because he will always do the job better and quicker than we can ever hope to do. I praise Him for that.

"CHRISTMAS TIME"

At the end of the year most of us celebrate not just Christs birthday but the end of another year of hard work and much overcoming as we have faced those difficult times which come to all of us.

Many have grief, sadness, sin and sorrow to deal with and these things often dampen what could have been an exciting time of enthusiastic celebration and great joy.

Yahoo, again we are getting to the place of planning parties, gift buying, and taking holidays {Even if it is just a one day trip somewhere.}

We are thinking what we are going to have for Christmas dinner {Even if it is just at home by ourselves.}

What heart ache do we have to deal with at this time?

What has happened at this time of the year in times gone past, and it is now the sad anniversary of that occasion?

What new things do we believe is going to be happening which is causing us great joy, even if we have a lot to do to be a real part of what is about to happen?

And now the obvious question; "What does this time of the year really mean specifically to each one of us?"

And question two; what efforts are we prepared to put into a renewed commitment to see and do all that our heavenly Father wants us to be and do in this particular tome of the year, in preparation for us to be more complete in actions and words for the brand new year just ahead of us?"

Of course we all know there is much debate around the world of when Christ was actually born, but in a way none of that matters.

What does matter is the fact that many people have had a hectic year and need time to rest, so why not incorporate that truth with the time of celebration of Christ's birth. If we hold Him forever in proper place, we should be able to incorporate Him and His will into and above all that we are and all that we do.

If we cannot do it that way then there is something definitely wrong with our plans and they should be changed enough to bring them back into divine alignment with the way and flow of Gods plans.

So let us continue to rejoice but just make sure who is in charge of all our plans and purposes;

Is it God or us?

"HEARING FROM OUR FATHER"

I think I would rather have the need of God speaking in my heart with words of; "It is time to slow down all the research you are doing, trust Me to give you the best help you could possibly ever need. I know the need of good information for the results for the efforts you put into each and every project. Now it is time to see what I can do for you which goes beyond all your ability of study"

Of course I acknowledge we need to have a little discipline even in the things which give us very real pleasure, as we learn about them. However we can get lost in the many hours and sometimes expense of things we do as preparation to do some specific new thing. Knowledge is a necessity in so many ways, but leaning on Him and his ability to give us new knowledge with His understanding and not just our own understanding alone is far greater.

{Ref 52} Leaning on the everlasting and ever loving arms of God, needs to be put into action with all that we are doing.

Faith in His blessed support and direction is just another way of allowing The Master of the universe to be part of all that we are doing. It is also a very healthy way of admitting we do not know everything and we definitely need His help. I am often reminded by our heavenly Father, that regardless to how well we can do something in our own effort, which may even appear to be perfect, when we invite Him to be a part of what we are doing, then things will always turn out to be a whole lot better than anything we could ever imagine let alone anything we can do.

I really praise Him for that fact.

{Ref 52} DEUTERONOMY 33; 27

"IT'S ALL BY FAITH"

As Gods children we are still living in human bodies, therefore we will at times find it quite difficult to do the things.

He asks of us.

Often we will have to step out in what appears to be unusual faith to fulfil our commitments to Him.

When we first make those commitments it seems so easy to carry them out. But some days we get tired then we know the testing of our words and our wills is in action.

Are we going to still make every effort to keep our words alive and going on in actions?

It is in those times without any form of condemnation at all we need to reach out to the only one who can help us through such times. When we are so tired we can hardly keep our eyes open; it's hard to reach out for others in real prayer with understanding and with the spirit. It's in those times we need to press in by faith and simply open our mouth as we consciously trust God to keep his word which says:

{Ref 53} For us to open your mouth and I will give you the words.

I am rarely so tired that I cannot pray, but on the occasions when I am I need to incorporate as many scriptures together as possible to become motivated in prayer again.

It's in those times when He keeps His word and by His spirit He brings to memory the most appropriate scriptures for that particular occasion.

It's in those times when His call for our sacrifice of praise needs to be put into action.

For a Christian; it's all by faith and not by feelings.

It is in those times when I see clearly it is Gods strength that will get me going again and not my own.

It's in those times as well as many, many other times when I give thanks to my heavenly Father that He is still with me and still loves me and hasn't given up on me.

{Ref 54} I will never give up on you

[Ref 53]; Luke 21:15+exodus 4:12+ezekial 3:27+matt 10:19

Ref 54. psalm 81:10

"DO WE HAVE ANY RATS IN OUR HOMES?"

We all know that rats are nasty, disease carrying, and not very nice.

Firstly they hurt when they bite. It stinks where they have been and they chew away and destroy everything they touch.

So we need to take proper measure to get rid of them.

In our lives' as Christians we also have a kind of a rat that comes to steal kill and destroy.

Wherever satan comes or any kind of his demonic powers their bite is dangerous and often fatal. That is so because they will always attempt to fill our minds with lying, diseased words, constantly attempting to destroy our peace of mind and the {entirety} that God gives us to live well with and successfully as his children.

The main place that is attacked by these rotten creatures {which are very real} is our mind first of all.

Satan always attempts to get us to be fretful, doubtful and give up on what The Father tells us is ours.

These attacks always leave a stink that tells us things aren't as beautiful as they should be.

Time in the word and large doses of humility mixed with a pinch of faith put forward with real words will destroy the rats and their insidious thoughts of lies which are destroying us and our walk with God.

"CAN YOU WAITE JUST A LITTLE LONGER?"

Sometimes we are troubled and condemn ourselves for having a sense of something hard with our inner man.

I would suggest we check it out with our heavenly Father before we decide to throw it out as something useless.

Sometimes we need a very long time for our loving Father God to cut and highly polish a precious gem which He plants seemingly as a solid rock in us and leaves it there. It can become seemingly as a thorn in the flesh.

It is a sure thing in these times of not understanding what He is doing with us that we are most likely to miss the point. We are not inclined to pick it up with joy and praise and recognition of its true meaning and worth that the thing which seems to be nothing more than a painful nuisance.

So can we wait just a little longer, till His time is right to show us with understanding, what He has given us?

Because I know one thing for sure, in His time He shall make all things beautiful and therefore it is well worth the effort of trusting and waiting.

"SOMETIMES"

As a child I had learnt how to cry in the dark
With fears and pains that had left their cruel mark
I would hide and retreat and go it alone
Till next I felt pain from some cruel stone

Sometimes I would hear you whisper to me
Come now my child and on me rely
I will gather each tear that falls from your eye
And store it in a bottle for eternity

Lord I've tried to be all you would ask
But found to do right was an impossible task
For anger and hatred filled my heart
How was I to make a real new start?

Then I would hear you whisper to me
Come now my child I will strengthen you
Then by faith you'll know just what to do
As you take one more step into glory

Often I attempted to walk your straight road
But lies in my ears and unworthiness too
The dirt from my sin kept me away from you
I needed to throw off my heavy load.

Then I would hear you whisper to me
Come now my child I will strengthen you
Then by faith you'll know just what to do
As you take one more step into glory.

Then you took me to your cross of love
My sin was cleansed, my load had gone
Since then your light on me has shone
And now I'm headed to my home above

Then I would hear you whisper to me
Come now my child I will strengthen you
So that by faith you'll know just what to do
As you take one more step into glory

Then as an eagle I learnt how to soar
Above high mountains, looking for more
But sometimes I have fallen to the ground
Still my Lord you knew where I was to be found

Then I would hear you whisper to me
Come now my child
I will strengthen you
So that by faith you'll know just what to do
As you take one more step into glory.

Come now my beloved and take my hand
As I show you more of the Promised Land
I'll give you the strength, provide all your needs
As you watch for new fruit, that has come from my seeds.

Now I hear as you speak clearly to me
Come now and follow wherever I lead
I know all the souls as you cry for their need
But first let me open their eyes to see.

"AT THE END OF EACH BATTLE"

NOW I SIT IN CALMNESS
AND FOR NOW NO LONGER BURNING
MY DOSE OF LIFE HAD SEEMED TOO LARGE
THUS I FELT I WOULD BURST FROM IT
NOW I SIT IN CALMNESS
ALL THIS AFTER LONG HARD JOURNEYS
CLIMBING OVER ROCKS AND UP MOUNTAIN SIDES
BRUSING MY BODY QUITE BADLY
NOW I SIT IN CALMNESS
AFTER MANY STORMS HAVE BLOWN ALL AROUND ME
MY MIND WAS TORN
AND EMOTIONS CONFUSED
MY HEART IN A THOUSAND PIECES
NOW I SIT IN CALMNESS KNOWING NOT
WHAT THE LONG NIGHT TIME WILL BRING
OR WHAT MY DREAMS SHALL HOLD
QUESTIONS, ANSWERS
OR A SIMPLE SWEET SURRENDER

NOW I SIT IN CALMNESS
WITH WONDERING OF TOMORROWS JOURNEY
IS THERE CHALLENGE
NEW ROADS TO WALK DOWN
WHO KNOWS?
BUT NOW I SIT IN CALMNESS
THANK YOU LORD.

"HE SAYS"

OUR FATHER SAYS TO US, I BELIEVE IN YOU
THOUGH YOU HAVE THE EYES OF A DOVE
GREAT TOWERING STRENGTH ABIDES IN YOU
AND THE GENTLE TOUCH OF AN INFANT CHILD
BUT THOSE FINGERS ARE JOINED
WITH KNUCKLES OF OUTSTANDING DISCTINCTION
NOT LOST IN SUBSERVIANT GENERALITY
AND IT'S IN YOUR SOUNDS OF SILENCE
I HEAR CRYS OF PAIN FROM YOUR INNER SELF
LIKE THE SEAS ROAR
COMING FROM GREAT DEPTHS
LIKE SOUNDS OF A VOLCANO
FROM THE DEPTHS OF THE EARTH
THEN I ANSWER YOU LORD
THEN BUT FOR A BRIEF MOMENT I
CAUGHT A GLIMPSE OF YOU
AS YOUR SHIP STEERED INTO THIS SANCTUARY
A PORT AWAY FROM LIFES STORMS
STILL YOUR JOURNEY WILL BE COMPLETED
AS THOSE GREATER WINGS
UNFURL INTO FULL FLIGHT
TAKING YOU TO NEW LANDS AND NEW KNOWLEDGE
THIS I KNOW, FOR I TOO
HAVE SILENTLY WEPT

BUT GROWN AGAIN IN, MIGHTY STRENGTH
AND I LEARNT TO SOAR EVEN HIGHER
THROUGH MANY STORMS AND RIGHT INTO
BRIGHT NEW PLACES BEFORE UNKNOWN

“WHEN WE LOOK AT NATURE THROUGH EYES OF REGRET”

“TO A SPARROW”
YOU CARRY NOT A HEART OF LEAD
FOR WORDS YOU WISH YOU HAD NOT SAID
YOU CRY NOT FOR A PRECIOUS LIFE
FOR YOU SEE WORDS OF YOURS
HAVE CAUSED SUCH STRIFE.
FREE JOY AND STRENGTH RIGHT TO THE END
AH, SIMPLE IS YOUR LIFE SMALL FRIEND
WHILE FLITTING ON FROM CRUMB TO CRUMB
NO DEEP REGRETS MAKE YOUR SENSES NUMB

But know this dear friend; we too can have total peace through the love and forgiveness of our dear saviour Jesus.

"MOUNTAINS"

OH MIGHTY MOUNTAINS
HOW GREAT AND TALL YOU ARE
YOUR ROOTS GO DEEP INTO THE EARTH
BUT IT'S ONLY YOUR HEIGHT AND BREADTH
ABOVE THE GROUND: WHICH MANKIND SEES

THOUGH YOUR HEART AND GLORY
HIDE MANY A MYSTERY
SOMETIMES I WONDER
IS IT DISGUST OR COMPASSION THAT YOIU FEEL
AS YOU WATCH MANS STRUGGLING EFFORTS
TO BUILD SOME KIND OF SECURITY
AND TO LEAVE HIS MARK ON SOCIETY

MANY STRIVE TO BE FAMOUS OR
EVEN BECOME HEROES
AFTER ALL, MAN DID WIN FOR A TIME
IN HIS BATTLE AGAINST MAN AND THE ELEMENTS
YOU ALLOW MEN AND ANIMALS TO TAKE REST
TO BUILD HOMES, TO BE A PART OF ALL THAT LIFE
WHICH YOU CONTINUALLY PROTECT
FROM MANY A STORM
BUT ULTIMATELY YOU OUTLAST THEM ALL

"AS WE STAND WATCHING THE MIGHTY OCEANS"

"SEA MISTS"

MAY THE MISTS THAT ROLL IN FROM THE SEA
SPANNING TIME AND ALL BARRIERS
BRING JOY AND FRIENDSHIP FOR YOU AND ME
OF WHICH WE CAN BE CARRIERS
AS WE SHARE IT WITH OTHERS

"AS WE TAKE IN THE HEALING OF THE ROSE OF SHARON"

WE'VE KNOWN GREAT PAIN AND
WE'VE KNOWN DEEP SORROW
BUT WELL KNOW JOY IN A NEW TOMORROW
PAIN IS THE BRIDGE WHICH JOINS US TO HIM
AS OUR BROKEN SOULS MEET WITH HIS LOVE
WHEN OUR STREAM IS FORMED
BY A BLEEDING HEART
AH, SUCH FINE INTERACTION THEN SHALL FLOW
TWO HANDS CAN REACH OUT
TOWARDS EACH OTHER
FINGERTIPS TOUCHING, BUT NOT GREED GRASPING
SOOTHING MANY HIDDEN MEMORIES
AS THEY STEM THE JUICES FROM
OUR CRUSHED SPIRITS.
NOW FRIEND, MAY THE PERFUME FROM
THAT CRUSHED ROSE
HELP TO PURIFY YOUR POISONED STREAM
AS IT BEGINS TO BUBBLE AGAIN,
SWEET AND CRYSTAL CLEAR
FREE FLOWING OUT TOWARDS THE MIGHTY SEA.

"A PLACE OF WORTH AND BEAUTY"

A PERSONS LIFE IS LIKE A GARDEN
AND YOURS IS NO EXCEPTION
SUCH RICHNESS IN BEAUTY AND GROWTH
WHICH DEFIES DESCRIPTION AND
ALL MAN'S MEASUREMENT
THOSE INCREDIBLE BLENDINGS OF COLOURS
RANGING FROM GREEN, BROWN, RED AND YELLOW
WITH ALL COMPLEMENTARY COLOURS
AND SHADED SURROUNDING
AND THE BLUE SKY ABOVE SHELTERING IT ALL
SO WALK THEN FRIEND AND BE STRONG
THERE ARE MANY STOPS ON THIS JOURNEY LONG
SOME MAY BE COLD, DARK AND LONELY
WITH NO FRIEND AROUND, BUT
STRONG SMELLS OF DEATH
AS MANY MEMORIES WHICH YOU THOUGHT,
WOULD BRING MUCH FRUIT AND JOY
SLOWLY FADE AND PILE UP
INTO SMELLY, MULCH WHICH YOU THOUGHT
THERE WAS NO USE FOR;
BUT REMEMBER
IT WILL NURTURE FUTURE NEW GROWTH
IN THOSE TIMES OTHERS MAY COME
MOCKING YOUR CHOICE OF VEGETATION

THEY TREAD CARELESSLY, BREAKING SMALL PLANTS
SOMETIMES EVEN TRYING TO STEAL THEM
THEN MOCKING YOUR CHOICES,
WHEN THEY FAIL TO DO SO
THEN THERE ARE OTHER TIMES
WHEN SOME WILL COME WITH CARE AND HELP
GENTLY WEEDING OUT THE HARMFUL WEEDS
CAREFULLY WATERING
WHEN YOU DONT HAVE THE STRENGTH OR TIME
OCASSIONALLY THEY PLANT SOME NEW THINGS TOO

THEN IN YOUR TIME OF BEING THE GARDNER
WALKING ON MOUNTAINS OF VICTORY
AND THROUGH VALLEYS OF DESPAIR
ONLY TILL YOU COME TO THE SPARKLING STREAMS
SURROUNDED BY BRIGHT NEW LIGHT
WHERE YOU RUN AND SING FOR JOY
AS YOU DISCOVER MUCH SURPRISING NEW GROWTH

AS YOU CONTINUE WALKING TO THE MUSIC OF LIFE
YOU FIND YOURSELF IN THAT SPECIAL PLACE
AT THE BOTTOM OF YOUR GARDEN
WHERE YOU RARELY TAKE OTHERS
HERE YOU TAKE ACCOUNT OF
THINGS GONE BY AND THE THINGS YET TO COME.

"IF I COULD"

IF I COULD CRY A THOUSAND TEARS
MY FRIEND I'D WASH YOU FREE
FROM ALL THE PAIN THAT YOU DID SEE
THROUGHOUT THESE MANY YEARS

IF I COULD OPEN UP MY HEART
DEAR FRIEND, TO YOU ALONE
I'D EASE YOUR MIND AND WARM YOUR HEART
ADD STRENGTH TO EVERY BONE.
IF I COULD WALK A MILLION MILES
MY FRIEND I'D BRING YOU SCHEMES
AND WEALTH ENOUGH, TO WORK
OUT ALL YOUR DREAMS
THUS CAUSING YOU MANY SMILES
IF I COULD PLANT A GARDEN FAIR
DEAR FRIEND THERE'D BE FOR YOU,
RARE PERFUME SUCH BEAUTY TOO
WITH PEACE AS YOU WALK THERE

IF I COULD PAINT A PICTURE WELL

DEAR FRIEND I'D SHOW YOU THIS
GREAT MOUNTAIN HEIGHTS AND GENTLE MISTS
FROM AN OCEANS QUIET SWELL

But since I am but one human being, let me say
this, reach out and take the hand of the dearest
friend ever to be found and trusted perfectly.

This friend is my very best beloved friend
and he wants to be yours too.

His name is Jesus

“ENCOURAGEMENT DESPITE ISOLATION”

Often we isolate ourselves from situations and even from the love of our Saviour Himself. However He never gives up on wooing us back to Himself and a safer track to finish the rest of our journey on.

But we need to reach out and receive what He will be offering us at the time, even if it looks odd to our way of thinking.

It pays to listen when He starts telling us:

"I DIDNT GIVE UP ON YOU"

A VAULT YOUR HEART HAS NOW BECOME,
WITH BRICKS OF PAIN WHICH MAKE YOU NUMB,
YOURE BEING LOCKED IN WOUNDS LIKE A KNIFE,
AND BEING CUT OFF, GRANTS NO NEW LIFE.

THEREFORE A GEM I BRING TO YOU
A GIFT OF LOVE AND FRIENDSHIP TOO
MANY SUCH GEMS ARE CUT FROM STONE
BUT FRIEND FOR YOU ONE STANDS ALONE.

IVE DUG TO DEPTHS WHICH I FELT BEST
ALL NORTH AND SOUTH AND EAST AND WEST
I'VE CRIED ALONE MY HANDS WERE SOILED
FOR IN THE DARK HOURS I HAVE TOILED

BUT NOW I PLACE THIS GEM OF YOURS
WITHIN YOUR VAULT BEHIND LOCKED DOORS
THUS NOW MY JOY IS MORE COMPLETE
AS ONE SMALL NEED OF YOURS I MEET

Yes, He has feelings of joy and sadness for us too; it is good to remember we are not the only ones who feel things.

"MY SILVER BIRD MEMORIES"

One day while I was out walking, just for fun, the clouds overhead would not let the day's warmth through. Then looking up I saw the mighty haloed sun and my heart broke with pain that was not new.

I saw an eagle there, all silver glow outlined as its awesome wingspan far outstretched the sun's rays, which made the great bird look like see through gold refined.

It made me ponder hope held out in bygone days.

A friend and I had shared a song of strength which filled our emotional streams with renewed energy.

I'd offered him a bridge to cross in his pain filled times.

He had declined the offer and now it was the great bird's time to fulfil the dreams that I could not fulfil for him and others as I let go of the struggle and allow the great Spirit of God to do what I couldn't and simply remember with these few lines, I tried.

"JUST IMAGINE FOR A MOMENT IF A ROSE COULD TALK"

THOUGH I WAS PICKED ON A MORNING SO COLD
STILL MY LOVE AND PERFUME REACH OUT TO YOU
FOR THEY COME NOT FROM THE COLD WIND
BUT FROM THE NURTURE OF THE SUNSHINE
AND THERE ARE MANY MORE THINGS
WHICH CANNOT BE TOLD.

I WAS PICKED WITH HANDS THAT
LOVED ME AND CARED
AFTER I WAS THOUGHT ABOUT CAREFULLY
BUT MANY OF MY FRIENDS WERE BROKEN SHORT
FOR THE WIND HAD PLAYED A LITTLE TOO HARD
SO NOW I AM YOURS THROUGH
LOVE THAT IS SHARED.
HOLD ME CLOSE THEN, AND TOUCH
MY PETALS TENDERLY
PUSH ME FAR AWAY, OR FORGET I AM THERE
CRUSH ME AND YOU WILL STILL KNOW FORGIVENESS
AS MY PEERFUME FILLS THE AIR
SOON NOW MY LIFE WILL FADE
SO THEN,

MAY I BE ANOTHER OF YOUR MEMORIES OF BEAUTY

"THIS IS FOR WHEN WE MAKE GEOGRAPHICAL
OR ANY OTHER KIND OF CHANGE,
WHICH CHANGES OUR LIVES."

"BEGIN AGAIN"

YES IT'S A NEW TIME AND A NEW START
YOURE LEARNING TO CLIMB
SOME GREAT NEW SLOPES
MAY FULLNESS OF STRENGTH BE IN YOUR HEART
AND GIVE YOU FRESH NEW SEASONS
AND BRIGHT NEW HOPES.

"GOD IS DEFINATELY A GOD OF JUSTICE,
TRUTH, POWER, HOLINESS, MERCY,
TENDERNESS AND AWESOME AUTHORITY"
"BUT STILL; WHAT ABOUT"

"INTIMATE SHARING"

But how would it be to share with him, as an act of worship a little of the poetic beauty we feel. Especially on the occasions when there is no one else to share it with, while it is actually happening.

Oh such golden splendour as the sun sets gently on the horizon.

I hear waves gently slapping on the shore.

I see Seagulls by the hundreds on their homeward bound journey, yes and a few folk quietly and slowly strolling by.

Now the waves roll and cross over each other but not stopping each other's pattern of life.

One seagull stops closely beside me just looking, watching and wondering why I am there.

After a short while it begins to share its glances between myself and the sea.

The breeze softly caresses my arms and cheeks and plays with my hair reminding me; tomorrow it will still all be there.

I watch all this as night time watches me. For now it moves its cloak to hide all views from sight. Yet, still the words remain of one who spoke earlier;

"This same piece of water has been here for thousands of years"

But now I wonder is that piece of water more salted by the lives it has claimed. Is it more salted by the abundance of tears of many as they stood there weeping and watching the waves take their pain out and away to a faraway place.

The waves are splashing and keeping pace with the wind as it picks up speed.

It doesn't take much effort to hear their song as they sing. What was that I heard? Was it a promise perhaps of love and joy to share with all who come near?

Everything feels quite gentle now, even the sun behind me as it gives its last little bit of warmth for the day.

This feels like a small patch of paradise through which I have travelled on the same track many times before. There are tea trees in abundance surrounding that glorious spot, and oh the flowers with their wonderful colours of purple, white, yellow and cream. Their perfume is so strong and it encourages sweet dreams.

Spring time alone is the season to behold them for winter is too cold and dark to see them clearly enough. Summer time will scorch them and perhaps you and me too.

As the night settles in I see purple sea sponge that has come in with the tide. I see many hundreds of tiny shells all caught up in the seaweed that came in with it also.

Many fishermen who have been out there fishing for hours are packing up and going home.

I wonder how many fish they have been fortunate enough to catch.

Finally I too go home and am soon in bed almost asleep.

I am aware my day time eyes are closing as the eyes of memories open wide and my heart sings with thanksgiving of the things just seen heard, and enjoyed.

"For those who have been torn, used and abused and cast aside by man and satan and now feel perhaps there is nothing lovely left to hope for."

"A FATHERS LOVE"

MY BELOVED CHILD LET ME TELL
YOU ONE MORE TIME
HOW I HAVE LOVED YOU SINCE YOUR LIFE BEGAN
I PLANNED YOUR LIFE AND ALL ITS PATHS
THAT YOU WOULD NEED TO TAKE
YOU RIGHT THROUGH

OH MY FATHER I HEAR YOU NOW
A VOICE SO SWEET, SO CLEAN, SO TRUE
FOREVER CALLING TO COME FOLLOW YOU
BUT LORD, SO MANY TIMES I KNOW NOT HOW

MY CHILD YOU WERE NEVER TOO YOUNG
FOR YET ONE MORE STROKE OF THE MASTERS BRUSH
TO SHAPE THE FORM OF WHICH ANGELS SANG
AND THEN, STOOD BY, WITH A HOLY HUSH.
I WAS THERE AND LISTENED WHEN YOU CRIED
AS ON THE GROUND YOU WERE LEFT TO DIE.
BRUISED, DAMAGED, BROKEN, AND ABANDONED
SEE NOW, NO ONE CARES FOR YOU, SATAN LIED.
I WAS THERE READY TO MEND AND HEAL
BIT BY BIT YOU CAME TO KNOW MY NAME
NOW LET YOUR HEART IN MY HANDS BEAT
FOREVER STRONGLY AND WITHOUT SHAME

“SLOW DOWN”

SLOW DOWN SLOW DOWN
YOU’RE GOING TOO FAST
STOP RUNNING FROM GOD
AND YOU’RE HIDDEN PAST

HE COMES TO YOU NOW
WITH OUTSTRETCHED HANDS
AND LADEN WITH GIFTS
AND NOT HEAVY DEMANDS
SO UNLOCK AND OPEN YOUR WEARY HEART
FOR GOD WISHES
GOOD GIFTS TO IMPART.

"THE CHILDREN IN THE GARDEN"

Often I watch my friends working in their gardens and I actually envy them at times. I see their natural strength and their discipline and see the fruitful results at the end of their hard work.

Sometimes I see children run recklessly through their gardens. I see the damage done through their times of fun. It is quite difficult to stand and be silent in those moments especially if the garden happens to be mine.

I value the work I put into a nice garden whether it is a large or small one.

Children obviously have fun in the garden and I doubt they are even aware they are sometimes damaging the plants.

I am fretful and sometimes expect them to have the same level of understanding that I have as to the cost of such damage.

I am so glad dear God that the garden in glory land you have for me to run free in, is not controlled by fears of damage and destruction.

I can see you now Father just ahead of me beckoning me to come forward and enjoy the flowers and plants that I have not planted.

I am surprised to see such magnificence.

I am surprised to see things which I have never seen before

I know that all these things I have had no part in growing or caring for.

I see below some of them sparkling in the sun light, gold dust.

I see crystals scattered throughout the plants resting in the rich soil.

You tell me they are the tears which I had forgotten about over the past many years which I had shed in the darkness of night time.

The soil which they rest in I see has no weeds at all and is quite warm.

You are now and always have been the master of that garden.

I see many things which you have planted there in the times when I was simply seeking your face.

And I see I can run free there with you without fear of spoiling what you have grown.

Maybe now I will be freer: to invite others into Your garden where we can run and share together, without fear of damaging the precious things of great price there.

"JESUS"

JESUS, JESUS BY MY SIDE
DRAWING ME INTO THE BRIDE
FULL OF BEAUTY AND SIN FREE
WHAT A PRIVILEGE YOU GIVE ME

FATHER, FATHER UP ABOVE
GIVING ME YOUR PERFECT LOVE
LEADING ALWAYS BY YOUR POWER
EVERY MOMENT EVERY HOUR

HOLY SPIRIT BY YOUR FIRE
YOU MAKE A PLACE IN HEAVENS CHOIR
AS I'M CLOTHED IN RIGHTEOUSNESS
MY WHOLE BEING YOU TRULY BLESS

IN THAT PLACE I'LL LOOK AROUND
AND KNOW THOSE ONES WHO HAVE FOUND
THAT SAME PATH I CAME ALONG
THEN WE ALL SHALL SING THIS SONG

JESUS, JESUS BY MY SIDE
DRAWING ME INTO THE BRIDE
FULL OF BEAUTY AND SIN FREE
WHAT A PRIVILEGE YOU GIVE ME

"PERFECT LOVE"

I know Lord that I am not yet perfect, but I also know that your love for me is indeed perfect.

You say in your word that perfect love drives out all fear.

I know there have been many times when I have been cold and crouched over with fear, unable to move and step into the light.

It is in those times when I have felt as if I was in the back of a long dark cave.

Each time I sought your face with courage and commitment, your love entered further and further into the depths of my heart.

You have melted the fear in me and the coldness of heart that I have had towards you and some of the people in my life.

I am thankful that your love is a living thing.

I am thankful also it is active and strong enough

Ref 56; To DRIVE OUT ALL FEAR

THANK YOU LORD

{Ref 56}

“WISDOM OR FEAR”

IS IT WISDOM OR IS IT FEAR
WHICH STOPS OUR HANDS FROM REACHING
TO TOUCH ANOTHER, TO HOLD THEM
AND HAVE OUR TEARS RUN WITH THEIRS

FOR HOW CAN WE ENCOURAGE THEIR STRENGTH
IF NOT THROUGH LIVE INTERACTION
FOR EYES, HEARTS AND SOULS HAVE DIED
BUT NOW THEY STRIVE TO LIVE AGAIN

THOSE WALLS THAT THEY HAVE BUILT SO HIGH
BECAUSE GREAT PAIN HAS CRUSHED THEM SO
AS THEY TIMIDLY TRY TO DRIVE OUT FEARS
WHILE THOUGHTS RACE AND CROWD THEIR MIND

HOW MUCH PAIN MUST FOLK BEAR ALONE
BEFORE WE SEE IT IN THEIR EYES?
SO TOUCH THEM, TAKE THEIR HAND AND WALK
HELP THEM KNOW THEY CAN
STILL BREAK THROUGH

"101 BUTTERFLYS"

Approximately ten years ago I felt strongly our heavenly Father was asking me to do an embroider project as a contact point of faith as I interceded for who and what He wanted. I believed I was to draw one hundred and one butterflies onto material and embroider them in the colours he would show me. I wondered at the shape they were to be in, for there are so many different shapes and sizes of those wonderfully beautiful creatures. He reminded me where I had put a smallish butterfly from a wind mobile. I went to the exact place found the mobile and used the butterfly shape. I began to embroider the butterflies which were all done in the privacy of fellowship with my heavenly Father. A woman who belonged to a church which I did not fellowship at came to me one day and said rather nervously;" God has spoken to me and told me to give you this money to assist you with the project of obedience which you have begun." She did not know what I was doing and in fact she did not know me personally either.

She had walked and talked with God for two weeks before she was sure it's what God really wanted. She had never done anything like it before and that was the reason for her nervousness.

Another lady came to me with some unusual colours of thread and said God had told her to bring them to me because I was in the middle of doing something at his request. I was allowed to share the fact I was doing many butterflies but was never to work them in front of any one. Still the few folks who knew what I was doing after a while, began to ask how the project was going and how many had I done. I counted them and share the number with the first enquirer. When the second asked about it I counted them again, for I knew I had done at least six more. Some were missing. Yes, that's right some had disappeared off the material. I was feeling disappointed, heartbroken and a little angry to say the least. So all in all I had four different people counting them from time to time, without ever telling them how many I believed should have been there as I continued to work them. After about six months or so I felt The Lord was also asking to embroider many other large butterflies approximately a metre square. Some were embroidered and some were done with pearls, crystals and other smaller beads. I felt as though I would never leave that place of intercession as I worked through the embroidery. The large butterflies seemed to go unusually fast and over the period of five years I actually did at least six of the one metre by one metre ones. Everyone was done as I stitched each stitch in faith to reverse a curse and pray in a blessing at the same time. I only did the colours or prayed specifics as I was lead by the Holy Spirit.

I became quite despondent at the fact so many of the smaller ones were continuing to disappear off the material. By the time I finished the whole project approximately fifty seven had disappeared altogether over the time of working them. I spoke of this to one of the ladies who had been led to give me some threads, and wondered if perhaps I was not doing a good enough job so that God had to destroy them. My friend was a little concerned at that. She asked if I had not done them as an act of worship unto the lord to which I answered "Yes of course I did" Well she responded, don't you think God took you at your word and accepted them, I believe he has taken them unto himself and sent them somewhere else as treasures. Hearing those words broke the sadness and questioning, and then the whole project was finished not long after that.

Over the five years of working them, I knew they would not all fit in my house and felt to release them to missionary groups of people I had become recently acquainted with. Many of my butterflies went overseas and given to people who were building and starting new churches. One in particular was put up on the wall of a half built church before the service began. While they were worshipping, many real, brightly coloured butterflies came and rested on the butterflies I had done. What a glorious blessing that was to hear about it.

In some way I felt as if it was healing oil for my disappointment, about the ones which I did not know where they went to.

Why the butterflies disappeared and why the many coloured ones came in and rested on others I had embroidered I do not know. But I do know this much; Every act of true obedience, especially when it has meant stepping out in faith from the first to the last step of the action, will always bring true blessing, whether we see and understand it here on earth or not.

Praise God.

"POURED OUT FOR AND BY HIM"

Some years ago as I stood holding the elements for communion in my hands as I had them raised up in worship, I was shocked at what happened.

I forgot that I was holding anything in my hands and had them raised high. When the worship time was nearly finished I looked down at my hands and realised with a horrible shock that I had spilt the grape juice all down the front of my pale yellow suit; especially the skirt. I cried and felt dirty and clumsy. What would people think of me and so on? The lord spoke quite clearly and said "Do not put your glass down. Hold on to it and just keep on worshipping me." I did so and opened my eyes again at the completion of worship. I was further shocked to see my glass was filled to the brim, where as it was only half full before with the grape juice. He told me to look carefully and closely at the top of the liquid and I could clearly see there was a film on top of it, just like there is with most good quality wines. I had not had much to do with wines or other alcohol drinks up to that time, but I could tell it was definitely wine and not just grape juice. I asked my Father what it was all about. He told me again quite clearly; "Just remember, throughout your life time there are going to be many times when you are totally emptied out. But do not worry; because I am going to fill you up again every time. But what I refill you with always be far better than what you have poured out.

This miracle has been brought back to me in so many different ways and so many different times. Each time He is reminding me

IT IS HE WHO WILL REFILL, REFRESH AND SUPPLY ALL MY NEEDS, not anyone or anything else. Oh how I praise Him for such deep encouragement. Bless Him.

"DESPISE NOT SMALL BEGINNINGS"

When it is spring time and the changes in the weather and the accompanying temperatures are drawing us outside we notice it clearly.

I guess in a way, for those that are able, it is great chance to celebrate the warmth, openness and new growth which we expect to happen at that time each year.

Of course we all have different ideas of what is exciting about new growth and what we should or should not have to do to produce it.

To sit out amongst nature that has been put there by a touch of the Master's hand, is to me totally humbling.

It is in those times that we realise we can do nothing to produce the beauty and majesty of all that is around us.

Adam and Eve were put in the Garden of Eden to tend to the plant and animal life, and we, as their children are asked to do the same, generally speaking. However we cannot actually create the things that live there.

As I sit facing a mighty river that has been dry for many years, but now flowing with a quiet power that no man can stop, I am in awe.

Many times it has been almost dry, you could see each and every rock and broken tree branch, yet now it is so full of water that I wonder what really lies at the bottom of it.

This makes me think with much thanksgiving of the many times how I have become quite empty through my times of pain, heartache, struggle and temptations.

Then right at the point of each of my needs, The Master calls

"Come my beloved and sit with me a while, I will give you rest and I will renew your strength. Then as you continue on with your journey you shall be just as full as that mighty river that you face and enjoy at this moment. Trust me in this and nothing, except yourself, shall ever be able to stop the flow of the spiritual river flowing out from you."

Natural man cannot stop the powerful flow of a natural full river, and even less so can natural man stop the flow of the mighty river of spiritual life.

The mouth of that particular river begins in the mountains and ends up with its journey flowing into the ocean.

The river of life flowing through us begins in the mountain of victory which is Jesus Christ himself, and should be ending up in the ocean of life which is filled with all His people of the earth.

The natural rivers give necessary life to all along its banks and far beyond. Without that water nothing would live.

How many people are perhaps dying off because we do not let enough of the river of life in us flow out to them. Natural river banks sometimes break because of the excess flow of rising waters and can cause severe destruction and at times even death to people and animals.

This makes me think of the need of our spiritual river banks to be the exact opposite to a natural river bank. We should be ready at all times to overflow and break all our boundaries or comfort zones as the Holy Spirit leads.

We need to do this and help wash away and destroy all the works and life forms which satan has planted in ourselves and the lives of those around us.

"HIDDEN WISDOM"

I have a beautiful plant in my garden which is called Solomon's seal.

I do not know where the plant or its name originated from.

It lays dormant through autumn and winter, in fact there is usually nothing above ground to even indicate that a plant lies below.

At first it grows long soft green leaves that look similar to fern branches.

Then it grows a beautiful row of small, white, bell shaped flowers underneath the spine of each leafy branch.

Because of the size of the leaves I would have expected to see much larger flowers on it.

I would have certainly have expected to see them growing more openly and boldly displaying themselves for all to see.

These flowers generally would not be seen unless you knew what you were looking for and then took the time to bend down and specifically investigate it.

I have often wondered why the flowers are not grown more openly and boldly above the leaves, where everyone could see and enjoy them without taking any extra effort.

I have wondered why the plant is called Solomon's seal.

Perhaps in some small way the answer is the same to both of these questions.

If we are to see what beautiful things God has got for us personally and indeed for others, and if we are to know the protection of the beautiful things he plants within us, we need to remain underneath the shadow of his wings.

Remaining under His protection shows our dependence on Him. This will help us to remain humble and not find it necessary to always be displaying what we wish others to admire and give us the credit for.

Outside of that loving protection we are likely to have the beauty of those delicate perhaps even fragile precious things spoilt by the dirt of the world.

Outside of that protection we are likely to be burnt and destroyed by the heat of satans attacks and the trials and temptations of this world.

These thoughts lead me to think that those tiny flowers have an unspoken wisdom, wisdom not thought of when considering the bolder flowers which grow and display their glory for all to see and openly admire.

Many precious things are planted deep within the privacy of our heart by the Lord just for Him and us personally to enjoy.

These things as are all things, always seen by The Master.

Sometimes we need to go and meditate on those apparently small but good things within us and give Him alone the thanks and glory for it.

Not all of the treasures in us are for the entertainment of the world generally and indeed not for the eyes of satan either.

Each of us has been designed differently. Some as mighty trees, some as tiny plants necessary to complete some part of the picture of God's creation, some perhaps even as tiny as a grain of sand.

But all of us are uniquely designed and equally important as each other to Him, for He has no favourites. He loves us all equally at all times.

Perhaps we are hurt and hurt others by the way we personally view ourselves; such as; I am this great plant or thing, or I am only this tiny grain of sand which is not as important as something that looks bigger.

Mostly speaking, what looks bigger is often something someone else has and we want it.

Who really wants to look smaller and supposedly less valued than another?

"PEARLS OF GREAT VALUE"

"OR SMALL THINGS OF NO VALUE"

The thought in the last writing brings us even closer to look at what we may miss out on if we are in too much of a hurry.

We can be greatly encouraged by this thought; every pearl has been started by a grain of sand by nature or the equivalent which has been put there in the shell by man.

Without the grain of sand or small thing that greatly irritates the creature in the shell, no pearl can ever be grown.

Every pearl has been grown from struggling against the pain so severe because of the intruding object that they spin a special substance called Narky around the thing which irritates it.

The best and the worst of pearls are always grown in silence and privacy of their own shell, hidden from the eyes of the world till their growth has been completed.

Every pearl cannot be seen or even known about unless it is first cut out of the shell by someone who knows what they are looking at and what they are doing.

Often, that fish then dies, and just for the sake of some human possessing it as a trophy of the suffering of something else.

So then, are we prepared to offer and surrender the tiniest thing we personally hold to be of great value within us, for the Lord to do with it exactly as he wants to.

This will often be the exact opposite of what we feel should be done.

Or do we want to project, without any effort or pain, some small thing which has not had the chance to grow into its fullness.

If we present a thing in our time and before Gods perfect timing, it will only ever be like a still born baby, lifeless and of no real value.

So for that reason, we need to hold close to our heart as we wait upon The Lord, the things that seem small to us even if we want them to be important in the eyes of others.

We need to do that at least till we find out from The Lord if those things are for public sharing or for personal enjoyment in fellowship alone with Him.

It is an interesting thing to remember with the growth of pearls;

The greater the pain the fish goes through, the fresher the flow of water and the greater the time the irritant is in the shell, then the greater the beauty and the value of the pearl shall be when it is finally cut out of the shell.

"PALM TREES"

There are three palm trees outside of my lounge room window.

I have my main desk at this window where I sit to do most of my writing and bible studies. In fact a great deal of studies, sewing, planning for craft work of many different kinds and embroidery is done seated here.

You may ask "So what is the big deal of having tree at your window?"

Well for a start, to my way of thinking they are a plant which should be planted in subtropical areas, in gardens where their owners can take good care of them while they create a type of tropical garden around them. Where I live there have often been water restrictions over the last few years and I no longer have the passion or energy for creating much of a garden to impress anyone in any particular way.

Secondly, these plants at the size of which they are, are beyond what I or my husband shall ever be able to afford.

These trees were given to us by someone who also had no energy left to create such a garden either.

Of course I do very much appreciate the wonderful gift of them and give my Lord thanks for them.

Whenever I see them I am amazed at how beautiful they are, and I humbly acknowledge that it is not in any way because of any special care I have taken of them.

Oh yes I or my husband do water them and keep any major weeds away from them, but apart from that they take good care of themselves; with God's help of course.

Having shared all that information the main issue is this;

They are beautiful plants but in an unusual place.

They are a great blessing which I do not really deserve.

But our dear God has seen fit to place this treasure or blessing in an unusual place for my continued pleasure.

It does not take long for me to think of many, many unusual things God has placed in my life for my pleasure.

Those things can be spiritual blessings of knowledge or understanding, or simply the many living things amongst nature.

Or they can be as simple as an unexpected smile on someone's face especially that of a Childs face looking up at you even though they don't know you.

It can indeed be unexpected things anywhere, any time in any and all aspects of our life.

As we begin to take some notice of these things, we soon see just how richly blessed we are.

We also see just how continuous Gods wonderful love is as He smiles upon us with favour.

"OPEN OUR EYES"

OPEN OUR EYES LORD
WE WANT TO SEE JESUS AND
WE WANT TO SEE ALL THAT YOU HAVE FOR US
BOTH SPIRITUAL AND NATURAL
THEN HELP US TO ACCEPT IT ALL
BUT ACCEPT IT WITH A HEART FILLED
WITH PRAISE AND THANKSGIVING.

Help us to recognise and give you the praise and honour especially for the things we cannot do or arrange for ourselves.

“HIDDEN TREASURES”

For many years I have been going to a particular beautiful gorge in a country town where my parents had been living and working many years previously.

I had walked through that gorge a few times by myself and at times with my two smaller children.

In those days I was quite a bit fitter and younger than I am now.

So myself and my husband and children spent a reasonable amount of time scrambling over rocks and investigating every nook and cranny, every crack and crevice.

Over twenty odd years later when my children had grown up and I had remarried I started going to that gorge again.

Sometimes just sitting and listening to the birds and smelling the beautiful bush smells, watching ants and birds coming closer all the time to see if I had any scraps of food to give them.

The weather was always a main factor as to how long we stayed there.

Because the whole gorge was basically made up of blue metal rocks, when it was hot it was quite uncomfortable.

When it was cold we had to sit in the car for a few minutes and then go home. Often we would take some fish and chips and sit watching the sun go down.

Those moments and hours have been some of the most beautiful times of my life.

Though I had been through that gorge many times with my first husband checking out all the rocks and plants and other aspects of nature, I had missed something special.

It was not till I had been through there a few times with my second husband investigating yet again some of the old rocks and so on that I discovered or perhaps I should say rediscovered a hidden treasure.

Behind one of the larger rocks which I had been over many times before, there was a lone plant which I quickly recognised as an Aram Lilly. I recognised it because it had one single white bloom on it.

This lone Lilly grew amongst the tall grasses which were hiding it. I was amazed to see it there at all after being there so many times over a period of over twenty years. I know I had seen the plant itself before but not taken much notice of it because I had never seen the flower on it before.

I went back to that place many times after that over the years and each time there was one more Lilly in that hidden patch of growth.

From the first time I saw it I could not help but give thanks to God for the exclusive enjoyment of any flowers at all being in that remote and now for me, now inaccessible place.

I have often wondered how the plant ever got there in the first place.

All I do know for sure is this;

Our Father God will plant or put things in areas where He alone knows we are going to go some day.

Even if it means we are the only ones who see or know where some things of beauty are. It also shows for us He will always have hidden treasures for us wherever we are.

Sometimes however we need His help to see the things we haven't been able to see before.

We all need to have our eyes cleansed, healed opened and anointed to see the things He has for us and wants to give freely to us.

We also need to remember the hidden treasures are not where we expect them to be, but where He has freely and lovingly placed them.

I suspect that most if not all of these hidden treasures are only found when we seek Him out for fellowship, or when we take time to follow that still small voice, which calls us aside, to simply be alone with Him.

"HEAL OUR EYES LORD"

Before our heart has been healed and made ready by The Holy Spirit, we cannot see that it is our God alone that provides all our spiritual needs and in fact is the source of all our supply. We may attempt many times to sit quietly with Him and seek His face out of love and worship, or for our needs. But how often do we go away from that quiet place feeling unheard and therefore unanswered?

Our hearts may even be bitter, more deeply hurting and possibly more unbelieving. As He heals and tenderly opens our spiritual eyes and enables us to see, we will be shocked beyond all measure just how much He has heard and has already answered.

We sit in that quiet place but often unaware that we have gone there with our attitudes of wanting to control the situation. We often expect Him to do a certain thing or provide a particular need our way and in our time, but because of His never ending, perfect love and understanding,

{Ref 57} His way and His timing will always be perfect.

By faith we are able to accept His wonderful provision if we continually accept the fact He alone has already made the roadway into fellowship with Him possible. Christ has done that once and for all by His perfect love and sacrifice on Calvary. He knows our human makeup, after all it was Him that designed us and gave each of us our individual personality. He knew we would struggle with the concept of trusting whole heartedly. However He still calls us each and every day "Come my beloved, come and sit with me before you set out to do all that the day is demanding of you."

When He calls us to sit with Him, I believe He also provides for us the seat to sit on with Him, the place to do it and the time we need.

{Ref 58} For we are seated with Him in heavenly places.

{Ref 57} Ecclesiastes 3:11

{Ref 58} Ephesians 2:6

"I SHALL SOAR"

I SHALL SOAR WITH MY GOD
TO HEIGHTS UNKNOWN
I SHALL SEE THINGS WHICH BEFORE
HE HAS NEVER SHOWN
"FROM A DREAM"

"ONLY HALF A BOWL FULL"

In this dream I had gone to a restaurant and approached a table I had been led to, expecting some exotic meal. After all I was going to be paying what I believed to be a high price for it.

Can you imagine my disgust when I discovered that there was not even a chair to sit on?

The table was only a very old dark wooden one without a tablecloth covering it and no cutlery set out to eat the food with.

There was nothing I could add to it to make it taste closer to my personal liking.

I stood there amazed at what seemed to be a total neglect towards me as a paying guest.

After what appeared to be a very long time, a man came quietly towards me and asked in a voice I could barely hear "Madam are you not happy with the meal I have especially prepared for you?" I wanted to be polite, so acted as if I was happy with the meal. Then he quietly said "Why haven't you at least tried to eat the meal if you are truly happy with it?" I was shocked at the fact he could see through my lies and wanted to walk out of the room and hide my embarrassment. He gently touched my arm and led me back to the table, only then did I see there was a glorious chair close by, totally covered in the most beautiful and unusual carving.

The to my shock I saw my name carved on the back rest with inlaid precious deep red gems used to highlight the colouring of it.

He held the chair for me as I sat down and considered eating the food in the bowl before me. As I touched the bowl and moved it a little close to me, I realised there was a spoon so close to it that it was touching my hand. As I lifted it and began to put it towards the bowl I saw that the bowl was actually quite full and not half empty as I initially thought.

The aroma coming from the bowl was quite familiar somehow to me and made me feel much hungrier than I realised I was.

What appeared at first to be a simple soup turned out to be a dish with vegetables and meat with beautiful brown sauces? The taste was unusually beautiful. It was filled with both sweet and savoury tastes at the same time, yet it was not what we would call sweet and sour.

I was amazed to see that although I had been eating for several minutes yet the bowl remained totally full.

After a long time I was well and truly satisfied and then suddenly the bowl emptied as if it had been tipped out.

I was peacefully sitting there thinking about what seemed to be a series of strange events.

After all, how was it possible for the bowl to be only half empty one moment then completely full the next?

How could it remain full to the top while I was hungry then instantly empty the moment I was full. How could a chair appear out of nowhere? And how was it possible to have my name carved in the back of it, I was a stranger to this man, he couldn't possibly know me, and how could it have such beautiful flowers filling in the middle with the deepest red rubies?

I noticed that the particular colour ruby was the same as the ones I had seen and desired for a very long time, even though I had personally never owned any.

The man who served my meal was by my side before I realised he had even moved.

He was offering me a small dish made of the same stuff the original bowl was made of.

As I looked at it, it seemed to glow a little and the whiteness of it grew even more intense moment by moment. I decided to accept the offer regardless to the fact I still felt quite full. I was a little embarrassed to accept it, because previously my mum had taught me good manners and etiquette, which included not eating anything beyond the feeling of a comfortable satisfaction.

I was further shocked at how the flavours continued to change while I was chewing the food.

However, as I was actually swallowing them the taste became the same as when I first placed them in my mouth.

Once more the man came to my side with a tall goblet made of rose gold. I accepted it straight away without embarrassment. All down the sides were engravings of small flowers and words which I could not understand.

When I touched the goblet it was very hot in my hand. I was concerned that the liquid would burn my mouth if I drank it straight away. But then the man softly spoke and said it would surprise me how cool it, the liquid would be if I would just take a small sip and see for myself.

Again I was shocked, the liquid was actually quite cold and the taste was strangely like wine and yet like milk at the same time.

I do not know how much time I had spent in that small place, which I had thought was a cafe.

I became consciously aware that I needed to go home and get on with doing the things I had left behind to be done some other time.

As I stood up and moved towards the front of the shop to pay for my meal then leave, I saw that I was now dressed in different clothes than when I had walked into the room.

I was again seriously shocked beyond everything my emotions could handle.

I began to collapse; once more the man was right there beside me and gently led me back to the beautiful chair.

Sit here for a while he whispered, there is a great deal I wish to talk to you about, things you were never ready for before.

As I sat down I noticed how tall he appeared and how thin I appeared to be.

The gown on me was glistening like diamonds amongst white rainbows.

The light of the rainbows danced all over me and indeed all over the walls and ceiling of the room too.

By then the man was sitting down too and as he opened his mouth I saw what appeared to be small flames flickering on his tongue but in fact never actually left his mouth.

As the words he began to speak to me left his mouth I could see many music notes dancing on the air.

I believed that I was confident enough in life generally to recognise where I was when I walked into what I thought was a normal cafe.

But now I realised that I was nothing more than a small child with no understanding of what was happening around me. To some degree fear was beginning to rise up within me and yet at the same time I was totally drawn to listen to what the man had begun to say.

He had been talking for a short while without me hearing most of what was being said. Still yet peace was flowing through my whole being and my ears began to hear the gently spoken words more clearly than any I remember hearing during my entire life.

At the same time as I looked around me, I realised there were a lot more things in the room than what my eyes had previously noticed.

Although there were beautiful colours and things of smooth shape, small and large sizes I could not distinguish any of them clearly.

Each time I attempted to recognise any of them they kept moving around and I said to the man "How can I possibly recognise and understand these things if I cannot see them clearly."

"One day you will, one day you will he whispered"

The man was still speaking but it seemed that I had never heard anyone speak like him before.

His words were quite different both in meaning and sound.

Finally after gazing at all the beautiful things around me, hungering for them and yet still not understanding what they were, I turned and looked at the man directly in the face. He was smiling at me with eyes that had a depth which appeared to go back to the beginning of time.

His hands were moving in the same motion of waves, and each time they came together in front of me.

He left there directly in front of me on the table, many small round things which were unfamiliar to me, yet I still had a hunger for more of them in some strange way.

They had the appearance of tiny brown balls with an unusual shine showing through in some places amongst what appeared to be dried blood.

Though they were covered with dirt I still hungered to pick them up and look closer at them while I held them in my own hands.

Once more I was too embarrassed to ask, just in case I appeared to be a too impolite, rude and greedy person.

I truly feared this man's disapproval. I wanted to appear to be in perfect control of myself and my world around me. I certainly wasn't going to let anyone see how frightened or how weak I could be.

After a short time of this strange mans conversation, I could no longer speak and realised that the small round balls were multiplying rapidly in number even though nothing and no one appeared to be touching them.

The man smiled at me in a different way now, and without him speaking any further I knew he wanted me to pick up the balls and look closer. My hands began to shake as I picked up the first few and began to cry uncontrollably.

I wanted to keep them even before I knew what they were.

When I have finished working with that broken and bleeding thing and what they were but still too afraid to ask.

They are yours if you want them was the song I heard coming to my ears like a gentle breeze.

I knew in my heart that I wanted all of them and not just some of them.

Yes he said they are all yours but you must pick them up yourself, I cannot do that for you.

What shall I put them in? I queried. Put your hand under the garment you wear around your shoulders and across the front of you and take out the first thing you find in there.

As I did so I found something warm and soft that previously I hadn't known was there. I drew it out and saw that it was broken in pieces, covered in the foulest smelling filth and dripping with fresh blood in some places.

I collapsed with fear, and when I awoke he was standing right by my side with a beautiful cloth made of the same substance as my gown. I could not move but uttered in a feeble voice "What is that cloth for"

It is yours if you will allow me to place it upon you.

The fear within stopped me from speaking and all I wanted to do was get up and run from that room.

He sat down again as he said, "Whenever you want me to and will allow it, I shall place this beautiful mantel upon your shoulders"

It has been made for you alone and it will fit perfectly"

By now the strange thing which I had taken from under my covering garment was on the table thumping as though it was trying to move away.

I was starting to feel strangely empty and becoming more afraid with each passing moment.

For a long time the man sat there quietly watching and then again began to speak in a whisper which I could hear clearer than any words I'd heard before.

I will help you put that back inside you under that cover, but will you let me put the pieces back together how they belong and are meant to be first.?"

And will you let me clean it and make it as bright as it is meant to be?"

Although I was still trembling, his words were making me calmer by the minute so I timidly gave him my permission to do so.

Here he said, hold this, and handed me one of the small brown balls.

As he did so the ball began to grow quite large, the dirt began to fall away and the white glowing colour of the object almost blinded me.

You will be able to pick up all these balls as you become ready and grow hungrier for them.

put it back where it belongs you will find there is a very large space in it to receive all the balls I place in front of you.

Again I stood as if to leave the room and moved towards the shop entrance so as I could pay for the food I had just eaten and to see if I could find the right person to pay for the beautiful garment which had been placed on me.

As I reached the doorway the strange man stood in front of me and held out his hands towards me.

I was puzzled and asked for the manager or the boss to pay my bill to.

I am the total owner of this place he replied.

I am only holding out my hand to you so I can lead you out to the proper way onto the road way in front of you.

I found it impossible to take hold of his hand because I had never before been used to anyone offering me their hand in such pure friendship, and for me still to feel safe to touch their hand, let alone allow them to lead me down a roadway.

I hoped he would not give up offering me his hand because deep down I wanted to try and trust that man to show me how to travel down any new roads that I may come to during my life time.

You cannot pay for the food you have eaten or the beautiful gown you are wearing, or the mantel which will be waiting for you when you are ready.

In this shop your money has no value at all. In fact in here, there is no legitimately known currency.

The gown you are wearing is made in only one place and you will never find out where that is, or what it is made of.

You will never be able to order another one, because only I have made them for each person as they were ready to come in here and allow me to put one upon them.

All these things you see in beautiful colour and quick flashes of shapes around you, will all be explained as you are ready to see them properly through eyes that have been made able to see the things of another world.

I had no words left that I could speak aloud, yet at the same time my mind was racing with many questions.

As I reached the door way and attempted to leave I was shocked and quite frightened. I no longer recognised the road in front of the shop. As a result, I had no idea which way I was supposed to turn.

The frame of the doorway was covered with very old and dead branches from a creeper that had grown there for many, many years. Long sharp thorns covered the creeper and I knew I would be badly scratched if I scraped myself on any of them.

Again the man offered me his hand to lead me out past the thorns of the old creeper and on to the clear road way.

Somehow I knew I was meant to understand what was happening around me but did not know how to learn about all of those things.

I turned to look back at the shop which I had just left and knew I was somehow in a place I had never seen before.

I opened my mouth to ask some questions of the man and he had already turned to go back into the shop.

At the same time he was whispering, I will teach you many things and give you all the answers you need, but you first of all need to be hungry enough to keep coming back here to talk to me and eat with me.

I did not know how often I would go there or how long I would be staying each time, but I did know I would be back again very soon. As I walked away I could hear him still whispering.

"Don't put the barriers of gates and thorn bushes over the thing which I have healed, which you now know to be your heart.

It is healed, yet if you are not careful you will take back the fear that close all doors to me the only one who can clean it again and put it into the proper place where it belongs amongst all the things of beauty and value in you and your life.

"DONT JUDGE A BOOK BY ITS COVER"

Some years ago, as a small child, I lived with my family in the middle of the bush at the edge of a tiny country town. My father was often away looking for work or working out in the bush felling trees for some company who needed timber for building.

Mother would be inside cooking, cleaning or looking after some of the many children. I would often go walking alone in the bush, always fascinated by the many different trees, smells sounds and colours. My main hobby was seeing just how many different bugs and insects I could gather and then release after counting them. One day I came into a clearing in the bush and was delightfully surprised to see one tree alone, a veritable paradise for any bug collector. It was amazing just how many different coloured bugs there were. Occasionally one of my brothers would come looking for me to come and have lunch, or whatever else the need was, back at the house. On one of our trips back to the house we came across an old house, so dilapidated that we thought no one lived in it. We scampered around the old yard for a short time, saw no one and decided to go home. Our voices and running around must have alerted the old man inside that someone else was nearby. Not long after that day he arrived at our back door singing out for someone to come and talk to him. I suppose, because mum was on her own with so many children to consider, she told us to say in the house and be quiet. All the old man wanted to do was talk. Mum would not allow him anywhere near the house; after all he was utterly filthy, with trousers held up with hay band from the bales of hay. His tattered jacket which barely held together in any part of it was held together at the front with a piece of fencing wire, and yes of course he really stunk.

After a short time mum ordered him to go away, which he did. I continued my many journeys out into the bush alone and my brothers continued when told to, go and bring me home.

One day not long after the man's visit we decided to go and have a close look at the old man's house for it held incredible fascination for us children. We wanted to know what was so dangerous about this man that mum had ordered us never to speak to or go anywhere near his house again. Soon we arrived near his place, but from another direction than we had tried before. I could see many very old fruit trees near his back veranda. There were huge purple plums and apples mostly. I was drawn by the size of the plums and the smell of hundreds of them fermenting on the ground as the flies hung around the sweet nectar of them.

I couldn't understand why so many plums were never touched or eaten especially when we kids were so hungry. I picked one up and ate it as the juices squashed all over my face painting it almost purple. The old man heard us earlier this time and came out to talk with us. The boys were frightened a bit, but at that time I wasn't. "Would you like to take home some of the fruit he asked us." The boys began to back away from the house and stood watching with open mouths wondering what dangerous thing he was going to do to any of us. "Come inside and talk a little while with me he pleaded." Finally the boys decided he might not have been as dangerous as they originally thought. As we began to step on to his veranda we squashed the plums that lay everywhere, walked through chook poo and many other objects of abandoned rubbish.

We decided we would only go in as far as the kitchen. I don't really think there were actually any other rooms anyway. Just one large room which would now be bulldozed down if it were anywhere near a town these days. There were a few old chairs and nothing else to sit on. In the middle of the room there was a large old table I think made of old tree logs. Chooks were in his sink and had messed over every inch of the room, the sink and the table. In fact some of the chooks were actually nesting in the sink which fascinated me so I went and played with them. The old man smiled and continued talking to the boys about the fruit and other things which I cannot remember after all these years. He finally convinced us to take home a few eggs and apples to feed our family; because, as he said, with so many children it would be very hard to feed them.

He then followed us home to make sure we got home ok and to ask mum if she would like to have some more of the apples, plums and eggs at some future time for the children.

Mum grudgingly accepted the offer, but still would never allow him anywhere close to our house.

By this time I was beginning to feel quite sad for the old fellow and wondered who he had to talk to, who he had to help him clean the house and who he had to share all the fruit, and eggs and chooks with.

Not long after that my father had built a house further up the hill from where we lived. It was in the shape of a half round, old army hut like they used to have in the Second World War. It was made with corrugated iron. This new place became our amusement and I don't remember what happened to the old man, but we didn't see him much after we moved into the new place.

Whenever it rained we stayed on our beds for the day and simply watched the water as it ran through our hut which had no flooring. I can remember thinking that the old man's home was drier and more interesting than the new home we were now living in.

I shall never forget the bounty, the taste and the size of those beautiful plums. I shall never forget the buckets full of eggs that he brought to us a few times and I shall never forget the heartache I felt when he was never allowed to enter our home even when dad was home.

I hope and pray someone had at some time allowed him to enter their home whether he was washed and clean, or whether he cleared out the chickens from his one room house, or whether he ever cleaned up the many plums as they lay rotting on the ground all around his veranda.

I know we must all be safe and we all should try and keep ourselves clean and orderly in our homes and in our hearts;

{Ref 59}

BUT WHAT ABOUT THE ONES WHO ARE COVERED IN THE FOULEST SMELLING CLOTHES,

living in the foulest smelling houses and having no one welcome them inside their personal space.

{Ref 60}

Thankfully our loving Saviour will never turn one away when they come to Him, even before we are cleaned up and acting the way we expect each other to. By his amazing grace and his precious blood we are made clean; not by the judgement or fear of another.

{Ref 59} I Samuel 16:7 {Ref 60} John 6:36

"MY CAVE OF HOWLING WINDS"

There is much I do not understand about life and all its messages of understanding and the getting of wisdom. Before I got out of bed this morning I could see myself sitting in a cave at the edge of the ocean. As I looked closer at the picture I could see and clearly hear many howling winds trying to tear their way into the cave and throw me about. It was then that I realised I was also using the cave as a place to hide in and not just to keep dry and warm and safe till the storm had passed over.

I knew that if I remained there for too long the tide would have come in and drowned me. Because it was in a place that no one else was aware of I would not have been found in time to be saved and I would have drowned there. But you see, no one even knew why I was there and maybe they did not have to know either. As I continued to sit there after dressing myself I could see a few butterflies seemingly casually fly in and around the cave where I was. Oddly enough the howling winds could not actually enter the cave but the delicate butterflies could quite easily, coming and going as they pleased and without effort or fear.

I uttered softly to the Lord; speak to me oh Lord that I too may grow in hearing you more consistently and that without fear.

I am in awe of life itself and I do believe I have probably been afraid of success far more than the fear of failure all my life. Even now as I sit writing I have a sense of the bigness of life within me and around me.

The reason this shakes me around and seriously stirs my inner man is because, at least for this moment of time; what if it is right and then what if I can't live up to it.

Before I used to fear what; what if what I say do or think is wrong, how bad I will appear to others or even to God himself.

Would He cut me off, would I be cast into eternal damnation because I dared to breathe something that was less than perfect? Would I harm anyone else because I did not perform in some perfect way?

Well today I need to look differently at life and what I am.

I have after all been asking God to help me be more like Him, to be more perfect and less likely to fail and less likely to do myself or anyone else harm because of my imperfections.

In some of the special times I have spent with Him I have also dared to ask; Please father show me some of the good things inside me as well. Admittedly I was somewhat hesitant with putting that request to Him as well, because once more what if I saw good stuff in there and was not able to live up to what I perceived was to be carried out into the openness of life and society.

What if, what if, what if? I believe this day is yet another new beginning.

Oh sure I have started over so many times before and failed miserably time and time again. But now I say to the doubting spirit; What if I succeed and do so in a mighty way, appearing to fly only with the timidity of a butterfly but in actual fact soaring aloft as on wings of a mighty eagle. I am learning there is not only responsibility in the life of a Christian, but there is joy and freedom and in a big way.

Regardless to how much we learn about life itself and how to overcome all kinds of fear successfully; we are only still barely scratching the surface of what God knows and what He has in store for us as his beloved children.

Not only the bad and harmful things need to be brought to the surface to be dealt with but so do the glorious good and beautiful things.

Praise God.

"ROADS"

In every year we have all had new roads to travel on, often not knowing where they were leading to or how they would end.

Occasionally we may have had a brief glimpse of where the road was heading and then suddenly it would disappear behind something which seemed impossible to deal with.

Still at least some of them we battled on and overcame the things which seemed impossible, and then we would go to the top of the mountain of victory. There were old roads to go further along as we grew into, maturity and in our God given ability to overcome. Again we would go to the top of sweet victory mountain and have some very special fellowship with our dear Lord. These are obviously called mountain top experiences.

Then there were the obvious times of deep valley experiences and occasionally a few smooth flat roads with bits and pieces to deal with along the way that were not so hard; and so we had a type of plateau experience.

Those were the times of travelling on an even and a little smoother while we were in preparation for the next part of the mountain that we were meant to be climbing,

It is a good thing to think here about how sometimes we wonder why we are not having more frequent mountain top experiences.

But for those special times, we have had to journey and grow through many things as an over comer, over a period of time. Going from the bottom to the top is not an instantaneous thing but a period of learning as we travel and go higher each time with Him.

If we had not been prepared properly by the Holy Spirit, we very well may have missed out on what was waiting for us at the top of each mountain. We may also have not been able to handle it very well at all and therefore not given God the glory, instead of taking the credit for ourselves.

All in all, God never left our side. He was always in all things with us and He never gave up on us during any of those different and difficult times. In Australia and many other countries it is usually hot in January because it is the middle of summer. We have by that time gone through the previous year working in one way or another with our paid jobs, in some kind of voluntary work, family or even some church work. We have all had our trying times and times of sadness, sorrow, heart ache and troubles of all kinds. Amongst them however there have also been positive and uplifting times for which we truly give thanks and praise to our God for. We therefore have looked forwards to the end of the year and what possible celebrations we can participate in with others as we prepare to celebrate the birthday of Jesus Christ our saviour. Then comes the beginning of the hot season which some of us are unable to handle very well. Sometimes we don't have a very positive outlook because of how we feel or because of what is actually happening in our lives or in the lives of those we love and care about. We are standing in January and we need to give thanks for what has been and look forwards to what is to be for the rest of the new twelve months ahead of us.

If we look too long at where we were and what we did in the past year then that is where we will remain locked into both spiritually and mentally.

We need by faith to look forwards into the New Year and all its potential to actually see where we are stepping into the newness of that bit of life just ahead of us.

The last year is finished and closed its doors to us and a whole new season is opening its doors to us in marvellous possibilities, all planned by The Lord himself.

He knows what's ahead of us as we face the beginning of the twelve months of the following BRAND NEW YEAR.

OH DEAR LORD PLEASE TAKE MY HAND
HELP ME NOW AS I TRY TO STAND
AT TIMES I'M WEARY AND CANNOT SEE
WHERE EACH NEW ROAD IS LEADING ME.

{Ref 61}

In all our ways acknowledge Him; and He will direct our paths.

{Ref 61} Proverbs 3:6

"FOUR SEASONS"

It would be good to give here what I feel to be an overview of the four seasons which come with each New Year both naturally and spiritually.

In both realms we have summer which has heat and then even more heat with all the accompanying irritations.

In that time we are in need of a lot more cool drinks to quench our thirst than in the less stressful, cooler times.

Most of us for the sake of comfort and better health adjust our eating habits by having lighter types of fresh food such as salads and so on during summer. We have our fans and cooling systems going most of the time, which includes night time as well. That is of course if we are fortunate enough to have such luxuries, for many folk do not have them. Many of us become quite sick with heat exhaustion.

Many, after the first few days of summer know the great displeasure of vigorous scratching which all too often leads to causing blisters and heat rash.

Many other bothersome things happen in summer time which is unique to that season alone. In many places one of the main things that accompany the hot season is often running out of an adequate supply of cool, free flowing water.

Of course we need a good supply of cool water in our everyday life for almost every action and need of our daily living.

Spiritual summer speaks of the trials and testings we definitely need to go through, in continuous cycles' and seasons.

Oh sure it is certainly true that we need to be tested to be able to become stronger in all things. But it also represents the absolute need to be purified by the loving fire of the Holy Spirit of God, just like gold. Gold is totally melted by the extreme heat which is obviously much higher than heat for normal purposes. It needs the hot harsh treatment to soften it and make it more pliable for crafting something of a specific design. But more importantly it is needed to bring all the rubbish to the surface which is then scooped off before the metal goes cold again.

We humans are like this too; we have a definite need to have all garbage of our fallen character brought to the surface. We need it done in a particular way which only Gods holy and loving spirit can do. When He scoops the garbage out of us in our surrendered and melted state, then each of us are of even more value than much fine gold; more than all the gold in the universe. Then we shall shine and be more able to be made into some of the most glorious vessels of honour imaginable, perfectly fit for the Lords glory and heavenly use here on earth.

Then we come to autumn.

Perhaps in some ways autumn is one of the most visibly, dramatic seasons, because of the many changes of colours. This colour changing is most obvious with the leaves on many trees, but not all of them.

As I have at times previously mentioned how autumn becomes much cooler. Then one of the major differences we actually see is the falling of millions of leaves on so many small trees of all sizes. This is the normal thing for those trees. Many people actually travel many miles to many different places as tourists especially to see the beauty of the leaves during their many changes in colour and as they begin to fall to the ground.

There are places which have festivals at such times because of the dramatic changes in colour which boldly display themselves each year.

I have always been fascinated with such beauty and change but didn't know for many years why or how such a phenomenal thing happened.

Throughout the rest of the whole year the leaves are actually absorbing the toxins and filth of the air around them, especially so, with the trees with broader leaves

The changing of colours shows the leaves have absorbed as much toxins and pollutants' as they are able to handle and they are now preparing to die and fall to the ground because of the overload.

They have reached their limit of absorbing pollutants' and purifying the air for the many others around them and their time has come to die. So in their thousands they rapidly begin to fall, especially during the times of harsh winds.

Many folks become annoyed that here is so much rubbish on the ground as they begin to rake them into piles and use them as compost or simply burn them.

The leaves become an annoyance to many folk once they are on the ground but while they remain on the trees we all give them the great credit for their beauty and the shade they give. Many have written songs or poetry about them.

We have the general understanding that it is good to have trees around to create good air for us, but I didn't know previously that the leaves had to pay such a price for our human benefit.

Oh yes it is all a part of God's plan that they live and die for our benefit.

And that is exactly what happened when our blessed saviour came to earth and lived a good life as he showed much beautiful fruit and gave much shade for our benefit.

But then, when He had absorbed all the filth and pain and incredible abuse from so many, then he became "sin for our sake". He absorbed all the filth of our sin which is the equivalent to spiritual toxins. He came and lived for our benefit. Then He died and was buried; equivalent to the leaves falling to the ground, also for our benefit and freedom of access of intimate fellowship in the throne room of our dear father God.

Whether we like it or not, we needed Him to die for us as a perfect sacrifice, so we could go on living throughout all the changes and all the seasons we have in our life. We also needed the purified air of the Holy Spirit to be given for the strength we will always need, simply to live well in and for Him.

In out times of spiritual autumn we too need to shed all the toxic things of this world and satans filthy ways we have absorbed into our lives. Just like the trees we also need to rest to an extent, as we recuperate from what seems to be hectic and deep dealings of the heat of God's holy fire. It is encouraging to be reminded that all things done by Him are done in mercy, in His perfect timing, and in His way which is always the best way.

{Ref 62}

For only He knows the truth of how much we can handle. Only He knows what and when it is the best timing for us to do so. Only He knows what the best is really for us in all things and at all times.

The recuperation of which I speak is of course so we can regain more strength to continue with more growth and purification, and not to be used as a copout from life and all that it holds for us.

{Ref 63}

God is merciful; all things only last for a season.

But all this reminds us of what our dear Saviour did for us; He paid the price of death for all sin so that we would not be lost forever in the filth and the penalty of death for it. He died just like the leaves and fell to the ground as He was buried in the tomb. Of course I give all the glory and much thanksgiving to Him for all that He has done for all of us generally and for me individually.

Another of the things that happens in the natural season of autumn is the pruning of dead wood and sometimes good wood.

{Ref 64}

But all pruning is done purely so that all the remaining branches will grow bigger and better. It is done to allow growing a greater and better abundance of bigger and better good fruit.

"THEN WE COME TO WINTER"

Temperatures begin to drop dramatically in most places. We get our warmer clothing out, snuggle up under more blankets of a night time, get closer to the fire or heating system as we worry about the power bills that are bound to come in with more to pay. We eat hotter and sometimes heavier food than in the hotter months.

In our spiritual winter we are meant to stay active in life and in Christ but it is different then. A lot of working in us is done in the secret parts of our being, which lays hidden in our innermost depths. But we can and should turn to our God to keep our heat at a good level so that we don't become too cold in Him and just die off.

Oh for sure we are going to be looked at by many people in these times and be considered as dead anyway.

Oh come on they will say, they are dead, let's just forget about them. But the Master doesn't forget about us at any time and only He knows the full true and depth of our heart anyway, and what is truly happening there hidden from the sight of everyone except His eyes alone.

Still we do have need of these times. In those times some of the most powerful and precious works are done in our souls as we are made to be more and more like Him.

Winter is when everything goes the opposite way of summer. Rain normally falls in great abundance. This happens sometimes to the extent of serious flooding. That is when we have serious damage to people, properties and possessions. In many places many waters freeze and people go ice skating. Snow falls and other folks go skiing. Pipes freeze over and water no longer flows.

Not much growth happens in that time. In fact many bulbs and so on remain hidden in the depth of the cold ground. Unless someone knew where they were we would think "Oh well, they have died let's just forget about them The Masters love for us is the same as for all the temporarily hidden bulbs, he knows where they are and always knows exactly where we are.

{Ref 65}

Nothing is ever hidden from Him, neither the good nor the bad.

In the equivalent spiritual cold season we in fact have to check out our heating system, if we have any; does it still work? Are there any blockages in our fuel system which stops the heat and power of His spirit from flowing? Do we need any parts renewed for safety sake? Are there some repairs needed which only He can do for us, which can be done on the spot day or night without having to call in an expensive professional tradesman.

Have we got enough fuel? Now are we ready, now we have to make all the new arrangements to turn up the heat and stay warm.

Then we have the celebration one of the more obvious seasons of life; spring, glorious spring.

{Ref 65} Hebrews 4:13

And remember

{Ref 66} Ecclesiastes 3:1

"SPRING GLORIOUS SPRING"

What a miraculously different season this is. Oh for the glory and blessings because of a touch of the Master's hand as He brings to life, that entire purpose and growth for which He has prepared us for during the rest of the other seasons.

Blossoms and brand new leaves start to appear on trees. There is much new growth which has come from all our hard work and preparation with our plants and bushes. Soon we see full blooms flowering all around us as they burst forth into the new season and warmth of the present sunshine. Tiny new fruits begin growing on trees, plants and bushes. Bulbs push their way up through the cold soil where they were hidden during winter. Everything has now become a lot greener. Attitudes are changing and most people have begun to speak and move around with a more positive hope that the new season has brought to them.

Then we are actually surprised and delighted at the same time.

We are surprised to see new life where we had forgotten many plants were, or perhaps we thought something had died and there was no longer any hope for it

We are delighted to see brighter skies and the warmth which follows and we begin to spend more time in the open air. Eventually we begin to think with some thanksgiving, of the times of pruning, of purifying fires, of times of rest in our cold times and the dry cracking up of our inner soil when we have spent too much time in our hot dry desert experiences. Then we remember that in those times of drying out our strength becomes wilted like trees and plants without enough of the living water. And we know that during those times we did not really bear much fruit at all.

We then sometimes begin to recognise some of the workings of the continual movement of God's Holy Spirit which has been at work in our deeper inner man all the time. Then we can and often do give many words of love and thanksgiving for all of His new seasons in our lives. We know they will eventually bring the fullness of fruit and His purpose which we were designed for, from the very beginning of time.

"STORMS"

As small children, often we had to make do with whatever instruments and implements that was available. Often that meant doubling up on what we used different things for.

For instance, there were many times when we did our dishes, did our washing and had our baths in the same one tin tub. On this particular night it was my turn again to do the dishes. When I had finished it was necessary to empty the tub so the rest of the children could have their baths and go to bed.

It was a wonderfully stormy night with thunder and lightning and rain, coming down by the bucket full as the expression goes. I opened our back door, stepped out from the house a small pace and threw the water out on to the ground.

Of course at that time I had absolutely no fear of any weather conditions. In fact I loved and still do the all surrounding power of God almighty during the times of storms and how the elements are so freely displayed for everyone to see.

My spirit soars now as much as it always has during such times and my great joy reaches the clouds within moments.

This particular night as the water left the tin tub lightening ran all the way back up it towards the tub. I was so thrilled I almost cried. I stood there in the storm and watched the power and majesty of life as a small wood frog hopped on to my left foot. I cried to think such a little creature was comfortable enough to sit there. I ran inside and blurted out my exciting news to my parents and other siblings.

Of course as parents, mother and father were so angry at me doing such a stupid thing as they called it, yelling about the danger and so forth.

My reason for sharing such an experience is this; of course we need to be wise and go through life being aware of how to do things and remain safe as we do so.

But the very real problem is this; how much fear have we been taught from others, to the extent where we hardly ever take even a few minor steps of faith to enjoy by faith many things which God so freely places at our disposal to enjoy and give thanks for.

Many folks literally run and hide under their bed just because it becomes a little windy. I understand the need to be and to stay safe, but there is far too much attitude in so many things of; "what if I am hurt? and so on. I would ask this question openly; "What if we actually enjoyed something instead of being afraid of it?" I reckon we would have so much more to give thanks to our heavenly Father for and so much more fun in life.

"ANZAC MARCHES"

All my life I have been around and been involved with countless men and women who have served their country in the armed services. Every one of them has a story to tell and yet so many of them do not share what they went through because they know it is another world far removed from the relative peace and quietness and freedom of civilian life. The pain of what they went through and what they saw is also a serious factor for remaining quiet.

In a small town where they have their Anzac march of honour every year, I stood by at one of those marches on the side walk watching and crying inwardly for their pain and losses they have all known and yet they still march in honour of those who didn't make it. They march also for the privilege they had to serve and protect theirs or someone else's land and freedom. I happened to be wearing a copy of a set of medals, which I had acquired for the right and appropriate reasons. An elderly gentleman came up to me and said "Hey, girly, come here and march with the rest of us." I blubbered out that I had no right to because I had not served overseas like the rest of them. "Oh girly you have every right to and I am personally inviting you to come and march with me. Come and stand in front of me here in this line." I did so and was shocked at what I instantly heard all around me. Because of some serious pain in my back, it was difficult to march down the main street of that town on that day. However, to my wonderment and joy I did not miss a beat or get out of step during the whole march.

After we returned back to the local R. S.L rooms I explained what I heard and saw as I marched, to the man who invited me to march with him. I gave details of the screams which I heard all around and the pain filled eyes and distorted faces of so many men. I thought I had perhaps to some degree lost my mind as I marched. The elderly gent said "No girly, for some reason you have just actually heard and seen some of what happened when we were in the open battle field. What you heard and saw was exactly what happened.

As Christians we cannot always see what is happening inside someone's broken heart but do we care enough, often enough to step beside someone and march a short way with them to honour what they have been through and encourage them to now keep on going. Can we get used to listening quietly as their silent cry's fill the air around us. Then can we take just a little time to say, I care? I believe we can, but yes it does take a little courage to feel and see someone else's pain and do something about it, even if that means just taking a few steps in their footsteps.

"LADY OF THE NIGHT"

Not all things which happen in the dark are evil or harmful.

Many things which The Lord does in us and for us are in effect done in the dark and awaiting for us to discover them by faith and give Him the appropriate thanksgiving and praise.

He often uses nature to teach us principles of life and even simply to bless us because He loves us so much.

I am a fortunate enough lady to have cacti of which the mother plant comes from China. I was given a piece of it many years ago and it has produced an abundance of blooms which have given such awesome blessings.

But its true and bountiful beauty happens only of a night time.

There are long stems of single buds which grow from the edge of some of the flat cacti parts. You see evidence of the blooms preparing to open some days before the grand event.

When the stems with the buds on have completely turned their faces to the sky in anticipation of the forth coming moon light, you know within a day or two they will open.

My particular cacti opens between ten and twelve o'clock with no perfume. Right on twelve o'clock the perfume is so strong it washes over everything around it, including your own nose if you are outside at the time, but is gone about two hours later. By ten o'clock the next morning, the flower is dead and once again hanging its head.

I remember well the first bloom it gave me to enjoy. I sat up most of the night just to see how large it would become before it started to close again. The blooms are quite large and every single one is an absolute treasure. Everyone is new all over again and I try to get to see all of them each year.

However, if I become so involved with TV, or anything else which causes me to forget about them and go to bed, I know disappointment the next morning. To see these wonderful specimens of the night I have to make the effort and sometimes have a little discipline to go out and look at them, or I will definitely miss out.

Often, our heavenly Father has done some special thing for us but we have to make the effort to step out of our comfort zones and take a look by faith to see what it is.

The cacti flowers, which are called either Lady of the night or moon lady do their thing and take no account as to whether I see them or not.

The treasures of the dark night have to have a light turned on to them before we can see and appreciate them. To photograph these wonderful flowers I have to turn on the light and make an effort, or miss out.

"LETTERS FROM THE FATHER"

LETTER 1

Have you ever desired to receive a personal and specific letter from Father God just for you alone? What would you like to hear from him?

Oh yes I know we have the bible to read and hear what he wants for us to be and do. And yes we have preachers to preach to us, and we have brothers and sisters in Christ to share with us. But do we pick up what He wants to say to us individually and simply because He loves us.

I wonder if any of His letters would sound anything like this.

Personally I think they would.

At the beginning of a New Year as we wait upon Him wondering what He wants us to do for the New Year just ahead of us, would He write something like this?

My child, you have just lived through another year. Well My child, how do you think you went in that time?

Do you think you were successful in the fulfilling of all that you expected from your personal heart's desire? Do you think you have succeeded in being strong and an over comer, because of all the so called honest effort you used? BE careful beloved one, it is not your strength you are supposed to be relying upon. But be not condemned, I am here to see that you are refreshed and renewed to face the all that the New Year holds for you.

Remember that I hold the whole year and the whole universe in My hand. Nothing of what I hold on to can ever escape my strength. I hold the whole world and that includes you and all your needs and desires, strengths and weaknesses, joys, heartaches, and victories.

You have been harsh on yourself in some of the ways; you expected to be perfect by now. You have also been a bit too harsh in what you have expected from others. They too are on a journey with Me. They too are still just learning just like you are.

So now let's take another look at some of the things you feel you have failed in.

You felt that you should have perfect thoughts all times, and you condemned yourself, because a strange thought or feeling raced through your mind, as you stepped near to many problems and heartaches.

You forgot so many times that it is not wrong to be tempted. It is harmful for you to entertain what has been spoken into your ears by the father of all liars, satan himself. You therefore missed the fact that those temptations have been actual attacks against you. You were attacked because you have made much effort to walk tall in righteousness with and for Me. You are tempted often I know that, and I your Heavenly Father have always and will always work together for good, like a fibre of strength, everything both good and bad in your life that comes against you. I will do it to cause you to grow and become a mighty warrior that overcomes through temptation.

Your sin life is not really the way you have thought for a long time. You are now growing in the way you think and act, more and more in the ways of righteousness.

It only becomes sin when you entertain the lies and then fall into the acting out of what satan has subtly suggested would be a fine thing of self satisfaction for you.

Look to my truths in all these attacks and see for a certainty what sin is and what has really no longer got anything to do with the new born again you.

The blood of my Son has cleansed you and set you free from the price you continually tell yourself you are not good enough to pay. But do you really know it as a living thing deep in your heart when you say "I don't want to try to do so again"

For with such an attempt you actually put aside what My son has already completed on your behalf.

Be not condemned therefore but rejoice in the fact that you are Mine and that you are already fully paid for.

Love from your heavenly Father.

{Ref 67}

LETTER 2

"GOD OF THE DAY AND GOD OF THE NIGHT"

My beloved child, did you know that I watched you last night as you slept and still smiled upon you with favour?" I have nothing so important that I must leave you at any time of emergency or any time of peace and not even with all other things that come with the normal living of every day. I wanted to be there with you by My own choice. I have always wanted to be right there with you, even before you realised you could talk to Me every day and expect to hear back from Me as a normal two way relationship. When you awake each morning, what do you think it is that stirs upon your heart, as you begin to plan what you shall do for that particular day? Sometimes when you think you are weak because you cannot remember the very first thought you are playing with in your mind, you begin to be angry at yourself for such undisciplined thoughts. You also often find that you cannot reach beyond what you personally can plan and control for the next few hours.

You have heard so many times how important it is to control your thoughts and you have tried to do so, with self improvement books and practicing all sorts of supposedly well known disciplines. Some of those so called disciplines are not from my kingdom or anything to do with My heart's desire for you. You are too often busy about what you can imagine or what you can control, yet I want to bless your mind with the sweetness and safety of the abundant fruit of my Spirit that dwells within you. I want to bring back to your mind the things which you have supposed to have been building up in your heart from the life of the living bread, my words. Tell me now child, do you care enough to stop doing it your way and attempt some real and specific time in the peace and the power of My words. There you shall learn how to rejoice as you have never done before, as you begin to see more clearly what direction I am really sending you in, and not the hazardous steps you have sometimes taken as you taught yourself in the ways of the world.

My beloved, next time that happens, try to remember that I have already told you what good things to think upon, things of good report etc.

More than that, there are many times when I simply want to tell you beautiful and specific things which can carry you through the day in ways you have not yet begun to imagine.

So calmly stop from time to time and ask me if there are things I want you to look at before you start getting involved with your pre planned day.

Love from your heavenly Father.

LETTER 3

"NO NEED TO GO DRY"

My beloved child, crystal clear is the streams I gave to flow through your whole being. They come from My mighty river of life.

Too often dear one, you are overly concerned as to how you look if you should happen to flow with the love of God running through your veins.

Just like the way your natural heart pumps out the blood on a regular basis, then so does My river of life flow? It flows while washing and cleansing all and giving life to all that it touches on the way through. But dear one, all your thoughts of proving yourself to people who shall never understand your true pattern of spiritual life, all your fears of being less than perfect and your doubts about life itself are blocking the flow of the river of life.

It's Just as a natural heart needs healthy, wide open veins for the blood to flow without overworking the surrounding, muscles and sometimes leading to certain death.

Then just as surely, you need to keep your spiritual veins clean for the flow of your spiritual blood which I have given in Christ as it goes through your spiritual heart. Your spiritual heart is to be My throne room as you have faith in Me alone.

If you do have faith in Me alone, that flow will cleanse and give strength and life to all that it touches, on its completing journey through you and your entire life.

Ref 68

"IT IS REALLY THERE"
IT IS THERE, DONT YOU KNOW?
COME MY CHILD JUST LET IT FLOW
FULL OF LIFE SO PURE AND CLEAR
TRUST ITS SOURCE FOR I AM NEAR

Love from your heavenly Father

[Ref 69} rev 22:1

LETTER 4

"SAFE TO LISTEN AND HEAR"

My child listen now, do you think you can hear the angels of heaven crying out to you. Do you think you might like to hear Me call you to come aside for a while and see what we shall enjoy together.

Can you hear what you believe to be true, those words that continually say, "Oh don't bother with all that garbage, God doesn't really talk to individuals at all, so don't bother trying to get close enough to listen".

My dear loved one, hear Me now, I am calling you at all times, "Come away my beloved." Come away from all that draws you into eternal death, eternal heartache, and weeping and wailing with gnashing of teeth. Dare to believe, I have already done everything that is needed for you to fully enter into all that I have for you.

How shall you ever know the fullness of the fruit and provision if you cannot even believe that I want to talk to you every day of your life?

You are unique, but it is always safe for all mankind to have a common faith as they dare to listen to Me. I shall never lead you off the straight and true track. But rather I shall always lead you further and further into all that is possible for you to fulfil in My plan and purposes.

Do you know what rare delights and what precious things are there waiting just for you individually? I shall never withdraw My promises to you. And so don't let men, or satan himself, deceive you with ugly lies about My treasures for you.

Love from your heavenly Father. {Ref 70} 1 Corinthians 2; 9

LETTER 5

"HE ALWAYS KNOWS OUR HIDDEN VALUE"

Now dear one, you have come to Me time and time again telling Me you have nothing to give Me as a special gift. I would ask you to look deep and trustingly at what lays hidden in your heart which you have never paid any attention to before.

Or, if you gave them any attention as being of any use to anyone, you were afraid they would not accept it, or even throw it back in your face so to speak and tell you they were of no use to them and then give it back to you.

So you pushed everything down to the point of death just in case it was not good enough.

Now I am telling you, wait till you have sought My face and asked me what to do with those words and actions of yours. Occasionally ask me where those words come from. Now you will frequently be surprised to hear Me tell you that all that is good within you, I have put there for My glory, for you to use and for the benefit of many others too.

That benefit will not always be seen by you. But have faith My child and do all in faith as you trust Me to direct your paths for giving and speaking. What do you think is the foundation of all those good things you want to try, and all those things you want to say? They are from my creation and placed in you because I trust you to use them to the fullest and best way you know how. As you do that, the talents will increase and you will have even more to give Me when I call you to accountability in Glory.

From your loving father

LETTER 6

"HIS GOOD MORNING GREETING"

Hello again, my beloved child, have you had a good day so far? And are you looking forward to the many little trails and treats that I want to share with you? Or do you still feel and think that you are not good enough to simply step out in faith and take a risk as you run and play with me in the highway of Glory. Why must you try and be in control of all that happens to you and for you throughout the whole day? Let go of that nasty control. It is taking up far too much of your time and effort and it actually blocks the way of My Glory rolling completely down the road preparing the way before you. I want to treat you to the many hidden and secret things I have laid up for you from the beginning of time, but you won't let me.

Just surrender the fear of losing control and let me show you the wonder of life as you have never seen it before. Come now and run and play with Me for a while as you see the tremendous things that are beginning to open up, just for you. Don't put it aside with any more weak excuse of wanting to serve others first.

Sometimes you are actually hiding behind service; to avoid facing all the sweetness I have for you personally. Do not be shy with Me, I already know you fully anyway and I have not turned my face away from you. Neither have I ignored or turned my heart away from your heart's desire to be close to Me.

So come now and enjoy our fellowship together as you allow Me to surprise you. Love from your heavenly Father.

LETTER 7

"GREATLY VALUED"

Hello my child, did you remember that I have told you, your hair is important to me at all times. Remember how I said I number all the hairs on your head, therefore don't you know that I have counted all of them. I would not take the time to count your hairs if they were not important to Me.

So, if it is important for Me to know the number of hairs on your head, then how much more so are you important to Me as a whole person?

With the love I have for you, not even the breadth of one hair can come between us.

I told you nothing can separate you from My love.

Why don't you take the time to slow down and come aside for a short time, just to enjoy the way I walk with you in all that you are and in all that you care about and enjoy.

Who do you think gave you those good desires and careful emotions and works that come so natural to you? I am the giver of all good things and keep all My promises to you and to all that hear and believe in and trust in Me.

Just take the time to step aside from all that you care about from time to time and see what great delights I have for you in My presence.

Love from your heavenly Father.

LETTER 8

"HE REALLY DOES TALK TO US"

Give careful attention to the words I have been gently whispering in your ear, dear one. (REF 71(for have I not said, be anxious for nothing. That certainly includes the things which make your heart a little cold even now.

Be anxious for nothing and give that care and that problem to Me and allow Me to be the one who brings it to pass, but in the right way and in the right time.

You cannot do any of the things you are fretful about so why carry it for so long and burden your heart with unnecessary guilt and weariness that borders on emotional and spiritual death.

I want to give you life not heartache. So let go the battle which is mine anyway.

Trust Me to care for those you are concerned about and let Me do the best of what they need, not just your limited version of their needs.

OPEN HANDS AND OPEN HEARTS
ARE ALL I REQUIRE OF YOU
JUST LET ME BE AND LET ME DO
WHAT IT TAKES TO MEND ALL PARTS
Love from your heavenly father.

{REF 71}

LETTER 9

"HE SEES OUR GROWTH"

My child you are now beginning to be the sort of person I want you to be and the sort of person you personally really want to be deep in your heart.

Trust Me to continue the journey for you and with you. You cannot begin to imagine how many turns and twists there are for you, even in this day set out before you. So how can you possibly know what lays ahead for tomorrow and all the rest of the days left in your life time?

Do not be fretful that you personally cannot plan all your days ahead. I am showing great mercy by not letting you know what is about to happen before you reach the next turn in your road. All you need to know is that I go before you and make the way clear. If you do not know the clear way then wait on Me and I will show you. I don't want you to stumble and fall as often as you have been. I want to protect the bones you use to walk over so many rough tracks going through all those trials.

Some of your trials you have put yourself through, but then I use them and work with them for your good. Don't you believe Me fully on that yet?

Just relax for a short time and see what I can reveal to you, for your own sake, as a weapon of warfare to use against the only true enemy of your soul, satan himself. Like I say, you will be surprised as you let go of the reins of your heart, just how much joy you can have in your life. Bless you my child. From your heavenly Father, that cares.

LETTER 10

"HE CONSTANTLY REMINDS AND ENCOURAGES US"

I have promised you that I will never leave you or forsake you. I see your attempts to live that way of believing. But so many times My children do the same thing; they still fall into the trap which satan has set for them. It is always another bondage forming whenever you begin to think this way

"Where has the blessed presence of my Father gone? I have never moved from you're side or from your heart. Learn to trust Me beyond all that you see, feel, think or hear. I am there always and wait for every moment you choose to spend with Me, just for the sake of being in My presence. I know you struggle at times to enter into fellowship with only Me on your mind, but are you prepared to do what it takes and spend the time that it needs to get used to such closeness and intimacy. You don't really have to run away from my heart beat. You may be quite surprised at the music that comes from the rhythm of my heart. You too can flow along with it, if only you could let go the rigid control of those things which consume your time and take so much energy. Can't you just let go before you are consumed with exhaustion and forced to drop everything, and call out to Me for the much needed refreshing.

I delight in hearing all the little and big things you wish to share and all the cares you have for others. But don't let concerns for others overtake the room in your heart which has been designed for worshipping and fellowshipping with me.

I will fill it but you must first let me.

From Your loving father.

LETTER 11

"HIS PLANS NOT JUST OUR OWN"

I know the promises I have given you, I know all the things which you have asked and am now waiting to come to pass. You are waiting for the right time and according to My plans and purposes before I can manifest them for you. But you continually lose sight of the fact that it is Me in control and not your own insignificant strength that causes you to ask according to your own impatience, after I have said to you "Yes it is yours, yes it is definitely coming but wait for My right timing."

You become anxious for no good reason, when I tell you to be anxious for nothing.

But still I see what you are doing and what it takes to bring you to a far more trusting place with me, you will have rest and like you have never imagined possible before.

From your loving Father.

LETTER 12

"HIS TENDER EMBRACE"

My right hand is over you and My left hand is under you so now turn to everything that is surrounding you and threatening your peace and declare to it that you are safe in the hands of The Almighty God.

Much of what you need in victory is up to you to take by force when necessary, but take it well my child. Take it in the confidence I have already given you. Take it in the authority which is yours in the name of Jesus. Did He not tell you that anything you asked according to My will, in His name, that I would give it to you? You do not ask anywhere near enough for what I can and am so willing to give you. For you, the only example is to ask barely enough to get by; I want to give you in every way, life and that more abundantly. When I give to you and you receive with praise and thanksgiving, others will come to know of it and in turn they too will come to me and receive what I have for them. That way many will come to me with recognition of what and who I am. Many will allow Me to give to them and so I shall receive much praise and honour as they lift their eyes to Me and raise their voices in thanksgiving. So would you deprive Me of all that, just by asking as small as possible?

Allow your faith to expand and ask big, be delighted in just how much I can give.

No, it is not selfish to ask abundantly in faith, just ask for the right reasons and be delighted at the flow on effect it will have for you. But just be sure to give Me all the praise and all the glory. I will not share My glory with another, but I will give all that I do for them from my riches in glory. Do you think it is salvation alone that I have for you? Does not any good father want to give good gifts to his children? Have not I said, none has ever seen or imagined what I have in store for you?

Just believe and act upon what I have shown you now. Go my child and be prepared to give the same encouragement to others as I have given to you my beloved one. Don't you care that you are minimising how much you allow Me to give you. I want to shower you with those blessings that are stored up for you personally.

Love from your heavenly father.

LETTER13

"DO WE TRUST HIM?"

Just trust Me, as I attempt to lead you further along the line of duty and righteousness in your everyday life. You have forgotten all the hidden treasures I have given you as you ventured out into each new step. You became tired and put down your bag of special treasures. You became tired of trying to look beyond all the pain and offenses to your tender heart.

I have awakened you each day and given you the chance to look at things through your cleansed eyes. But you still chose for a long time to see those tears as blinding pain from the enemy, and of no value. Each time that you cried in real honesty I opened your eyes anew and cleansed them with the very element of salted water which your pain caused. I told you that I would waste nothing, but indeed use everything together for your benefit, Well that includes the pain, the tears and even the recovery that you can always come to, in Me. I have your heart tenderly held in My hands. I do not pass that responsibility into another's hands. I do not rub out your name from where it is engraved in the palm of my hand. You are there forever.

So come now my child, rest in me, as you take your hands off the battle controlling the factors of your life. I promised you that I would do the battle for you, now watch and see what I shall do for you, yes even this day. I love you my child.

From your loving father.

LETTER 14

"THE FATHER ASKS"

Can you tell me child, when you last took time out totally, just to hear from me? And when was the last time you had the courage to try me and see what I can do for you. Especially during the times when you had given every bit of knowledge and effort to accomplish something you believed was of me? When was the last time you really surrendered everything of your self effort and left it alone, till I gave you the blessing, enough to see where you had actually gone wrong and had started to walk on the wrong track of life?

You were so busy attempting to accomplish what you believed was important. But you forgot to look and ask what I wanted you to do, even if it seemed unimportant to you at the time.

How do you know what fits into the needs of yourself and others, if you simply do not slow down long enough and often enough to ask and then listen for the answer and direction?

Often you let go of the exact element I have been waiting for you to bring to me to use on your behalf, but if you refuse to let it go then what can I do with it.

Surrendering it means giving up what you hold on to and your right to use it in your own way, which will only ever be a wasted and limited, outcome of what I can do with it.

Are you consumed with the attitude of being right at any cost? You are no less worthy when you take the humble and silent role where and when something seems to be demanding your perfect word, action or planning abilities.

Do not fret though; you have taken time enough to listen this time. Be encouraged to know what has been possible once will always be possible in Me. If I can sit upon your throne within your heart and go to the edge of all things with you but keep you in safe boundaries, then you will see all the possibilities of rest and pure direction that I alone can give you. But rest for now beloved child and let the times of the past remain in the past.

From your heavenly father.

LETTER 15

"BE CAREFUL"

Days come and days go, and so often you allow all the stress of the life of your past days clutter up your potential freedom and actions of today.

You too often allow all the joys of your yesterdays to clutter up your way, instead of being ready for the freshness of today to permeate your mind, heart and words with actions. I am the one, the master of all the supply and want to give to you continuously the bread and fresh life in the here and now.

Be careful my child, that you don't begin to be demanding for the things you are not even ready for yet. Be careful that you do not expect one thing from Me, when I see and know what is truly best for you in every moment of the present, especially when that is something different to what you expect. When you do that you become cross, angry, disappointed, restless and dissatisfied with what I am giving you. When I offer you something, I am always offering further open doors behind every gift of love and every piece of your provision.

From your heavenly father.

LETTER 16

"I PROMISE YOU"

My child, I watched your hearts cry, when you wrote this;

SOMETIMES EVEN THOUGH I CLIMB A WALL,
THEN THINK HOW GOOD I AM, TEN FOOT TALL,
IN MY PRIDE, I STUMBLE AND HURT MYSELF
AND PUT MY TREASURE BACK ON THE SHELF.

But my dear child, come again and see what good things I have for you in this day

You cannot control, or even imagine, the fullness of one part of any blessing, let alone the fullness of a whole thing I wish to give to you.

You cannot earn any of what I have for you, but in your sense of unworthiness which overcomes you so often, you cut off, what I am offering you.

Won't you take your hands off the measure of the things you think you are ready for and give me your sweet surrender and simply trust me.

I promise you, you will be delighted, shocked and unexplainably blessed.

I am always waiting to give you many good things of great value. I know exactly what you are ready for, and when you are ready to receive it all because I made you.

I do not offer what you cannot receive, look after, or manage in your life.

I see your struggle against the lies you have had whispered in your ears, direct from satan and many times through the words of other people around you.

I alone tell you this truth, I am the giver of all good gifts, because I want to show my love and favour and shine my glory through you, as you receive in faith, praise and thanksgiving.

Love From your heavenly father.

LETTER 17

"HE IS IN CONTROL"

My dear child, don't give up so easily when you see things around you changing, beyond your ability to keep up with it. Don't feel that you have to understand all that is happening just because I have given you a fleeting glimpse of some small part of my kingdom purpose.

I am, after all, the only one who is supposed to be in control. I have taken you thus far as on eagle's wings. I am the one who has lifted you up to soar and simply catch the wind of my spirit. I am the one who will always tell all that you need to know. Wait upon me and then if I do not reveal anything further to you, let go in praises and thanksgiving and trust Me to bring all to pass that I have promised.

You cannot ever take my place, of bringing to pass, the things which reveal my heavenly purpose, for the earth bound children of Adam.

I will open their eyes and their heart to receive, but only as they are made ready to see and hear, by my revelation and care, not as you fretfully attempt to apply the workings' of my spirit on and in their lives.

Do you hear all the cries in the dark as they painfully attempt to force themselves to work out my promises to them?

Do you hear all the translations of lies straight from the father of all liars, satan, as they attempt to straighten out their humanistic ways of believing?

Do you hear the painful birthing of new ideas as they bear heavenly fruit in their inner man?

No of course you don't.

Then be careful dear one, that you don't attempt to way lay them by your impatient efforts to speed up My plans and purposes.

I know that you care a great deal how many are suffering and aim at setting them free from all the harm and from all hard work and hard times. You want it to be so easy for them. But human emotions will only ever bring a small quick fix solution and will never leave them free to live through faith and trust in me alone.

I care for your efforts, but rest and trust in me more and more and see what a great delight I have in store for you individually and for others collectively as parts of the body

Just let go now and trust me.

Love from your heavenly father.

LETTER 18

"BEING PREPARED FOR HIS PURPOSES"

Hello my child, are you ready to hear all that I have for you during this day. Simply because you are my child and that I am your heavenly Father, means you are able to do all I ask of you and hear all that I say to you. I made you and know full well how you function. I would not ask more of you, than I have made you capable of.

Yes, you will always go through times of being tempted and tested.

You are tempered like metal for the readiness of warfare which I know you are headed for. This tempering is only done on metals which are specifically made for weapons and instruments of my use and purposes. I would not put something or someone through the fire unless they are made for it.

You are tested, for you to see that there are things within you which need to be honed and trained for my specific service. Again, only I know just how much you can go through for training and practical use. I am the one who puts into place all gifting, all purposes and all the parts which make up a whole vessel. Each of my vessels is strategically placed within My purpose to fulfil the things which I design for each of you. Do not be distressed with the seemingly unfilled places of honour and workings of My heavenly actions on earth.

Bless Me and praise Me in all things and trust Me at all times then rest in Me.

Love from your heavenly Father.

LETTER 19

"HE SEES AND KNOWS ALL"

I know what lays hidden in your heart. I know the treasures which you haven't begun to contemplate, let alone been able to ask yourself if you believe they are for real or not. Yes they are real and of far more value than you will ever be able to reckon on. The treasures I place in your heart are for you to know and enjoy this life here on earth. They are also for the beginning of tasting and seeing what is possible far above your own personal measure of what you think is in heavenly places.

Do not despair of being told, you are unable to measure, what lays waiting for you after your journey on earth.

I want you to know, I am taking good care of what belongs to you here in eternity with me. Those special things are designed specifically for you and for no other. Each man has his own treasures I have given and will give in the future also. You do not have to at any time give up your blessed spiritual treasure just so another can have something of me in their heart and life. I have enough for all.

I have plenty for all; none have to be denied the good things of My heavenly realm.

You are the caretaker of what I give you to be involved in. Yes you will always need to learn of and know my timing of when and how to share those good things. But if I wanted another to care for and enjoy those exact same things, then I would have given those things to them in the first place. Stop counting yourself as unworthy to do my bidding and to carry with love and care the things of importance which I tenderly place in your heart alone.

Love from your heavenly father.

LETTER 20

"LISTENING WITH OUR HEART NOT JUST OUR MIND"

My child, you came when I called you, but you came in your heart and you actually know the difference, don't you. I can now begin to speak clearly to you again. You have had to have the last time of testing because I am about to give you some of the new wine which you have longed for.

You had become too used to what you wanted to have as the new wine within. In fact you had replaced many times what I had placed in your cup to drink. I love you and I will be patient with you for you have much yet to learn about what you have thrown away, of the things I place in your life for you to know Me more thoroughly. I wish for truly intimate fellowship with you, but mostly you limit Me as to what you are used to in your own limited faith and from what you can control or understand. I want to give you more than you have ever imagined possible. You say you want to soar like a mighty eagle dear child, but are you really ready to see and participate when things are totally out of your control and beyond your understanding. I have waited and will continue to wait patiently for your maturity to reach a level of total trust, and believe me child it is happening. Your journey is definitely coming to a place of splendour as you view things from a height you have never been to before. You will be able to rise, soar, see and do as My child and friend, in ways that are holier and more powerful than all your imaginations have ever allowed you to previously attempt. Trust me, I know all these things and when it is best to put them into your activated vision and accountability. Bless you little one; do not pull back from being called little one like you did just now. You are small to Me, in the manner of Me being able to hold you fully covered in my hands, as I hold at the same time all that you bare and all that concerns your life of needs and activities.

Bless you my little one. Love from your heavenly father.

LETTER 21

"COME EVEN CLOSER"

My child, you are the one I am speaking to right now. I am not some stranger that you have never met before, so tell Me why you keep running away from My arm of protection, when all that I want for you and of you, is a little closer and more intimate time of sweet communion. You often look for treasure and sometimes find them. Yes, you do come with much rejoicing and thanksgiving of which I am pleased with. But dear one, you are still often limiting Me in what I can speak about with you.

How often I wanted to run and laugh with you, but you either put me on hold or turned everything off, because you personally do not understand it or can control it.

I want to take you to the places of prayer and promise that you have dreamed about as you slept, but never counted yourself worthy enough, once you awaken.

I am here ready to receive you in all your ways of faith and beauty which you have never fully accepted about yourself and enjoyed.

I tell you again now how much I love you and always have from the beginning of time.

The more you can accept that one point alone, then the more you will be able to hear from Me and often in the least expected ways and times.

I am the creator and author of your life story and the very story of time on earth. I am the one who has appointed those special times of you finding, embracing, and keeping the hidden and unusual treasures that have been appointed for you alone.

Come now and begin to gather to yourself, all that has become your destiny, including the gathering of pearls and many other kinds of treasures as well. I love you my child and don't forget all My ways and thoughts and promises are for your own blessed good and not for your harm. Do you really hear Me my child?

I love you with an everlasting love.

A love that is always unbroken and always untarnished.

Love from your heavenly Father.

LETTER 22

"TRAVELLING ONWARDS"

I am the one who directs your paths. Do not worry or be afraid when you step out in faith, to fulfil those actions of obedience I have placed in your heart and mind. I will never lead you astray or against My infallible word. Do not be concerned about the travelling on a new path which you have been surprised about. You have entered the beginning of a new way and you know I am the one who designed that way. Now let go of the fear and allow me to control the breaks you may have as you travel the full length of that journey.

I shall surprise you even further as you see what is at the place of each stopping and starting point. You will be blessed and abundantly surprised at how difficult some new things will appear to you and yet how easily you will move into them and the fullness of their abundance as the tasting and receiving of them begin to happen in a flowing manner.

You are the child of destiny I have placed in that particular place for a specific season. You are not the designer or sustainer of my will. I ask now; are you able to tell me what is going to happen tomorrow or even today?

No, you are not, but trust Me, I know all that is concerning you and your every tomorrow. I still know all that is at the end, at the beginning, and all that will encompass you throughout the entire journey of this time and place of newness and its eternal worth. My child, you are still in the palm of my hand, so trust what I shall cover you with to protect, comfort and encourage you, as I keep you warm in my love.

Love from your heavenly father

“TRACEY MARREE”

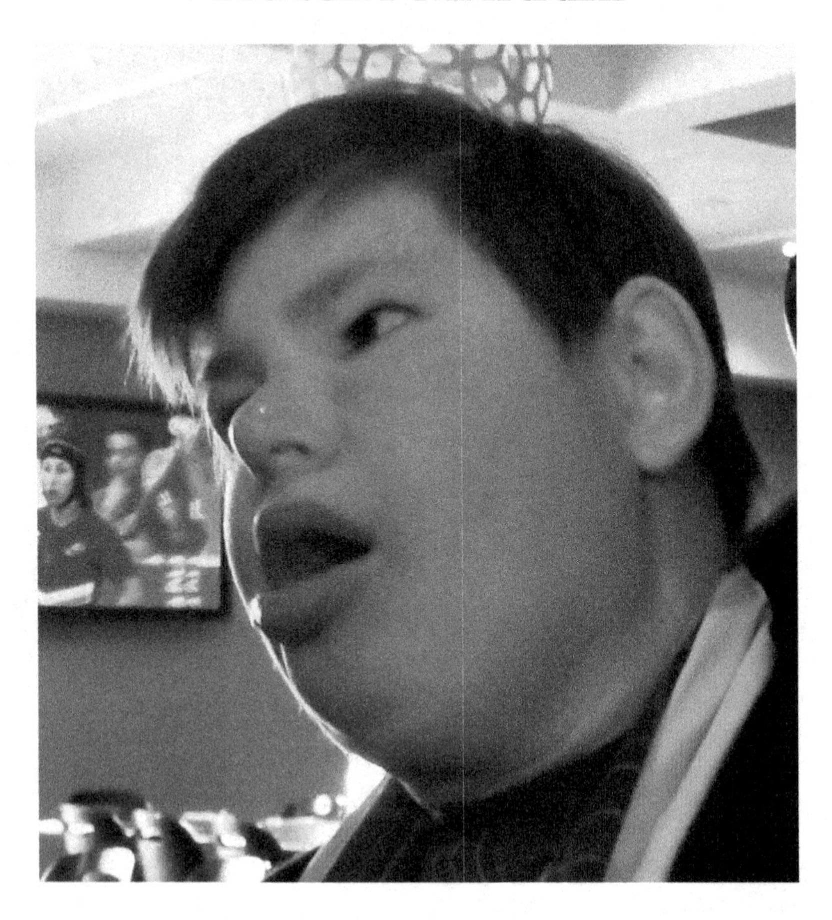

"MY BELOVED"
"LITTLE STORM RIDER"

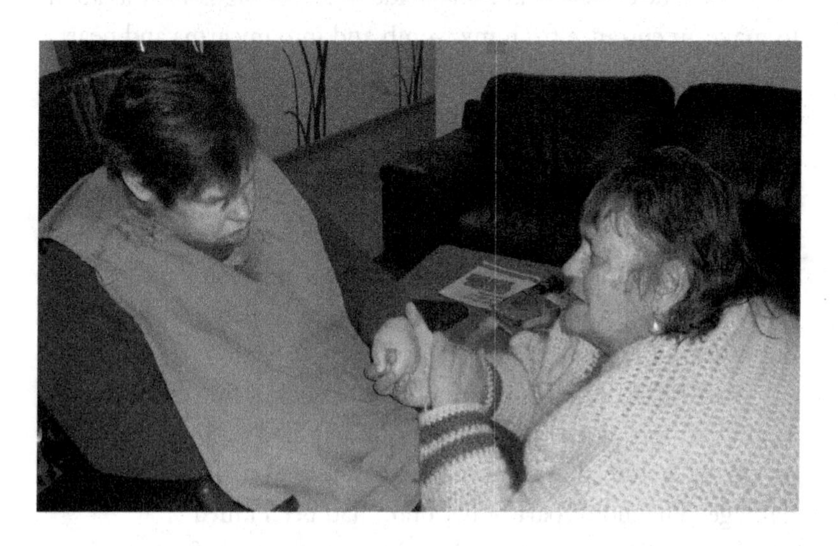

I waited forty six years for just this one
time of her holding my finger.

How does a person write of one of the greatest treasures they have ever been given by the great Jehovah?

How can we possibly ever expect that our mere words of thank you could be good enough for The King of Kings and Lord of Lords?

Honesty is always the greatest beginning of any story or sharing time.

Forty eight years ago, born through the partnership of love and marriage a small baby girl came into the world in a large city hospital.

I carried well except for an excess of fluid towards the end of the term. The day came and she made some real signs she was about to make an entrance from my womb and into my arms and heart.

She was ready and the medical staff was not. They forced the labour to stop for approximately forty minutes after both waters had broken. I realised afterwards what they had caused to happen was actually medical abuse and serious neglect of the baby and myself as they left me alone in the delivery room without any attending staff.

I was ignorant and trusted them way too much and didn't know how to pursue the matter legally so I remained silent for many years out of fear of reprisal.

Because of the way my princess was brought into the world she swallowed too much fluid and her lungs filled with water instead of air. Therefore she was born with severe and permanent brain damage. The motor part of her brain had been killed.

The medical neglect continued for many years afterwards.

Sometimes we can miss some of or all of what God is doing at the moment of our apparent heartbreaking happenings.

Six hours after she was born the matron came and told me she had another six hours to live and asked if I wanted her to be baptised to which I answered yes.

At the time I was a catholic and was therefore very interested in the rest of the procedures which the priest also carried out when he came, that is apart from what is known as the last rights.

I understood what he was doing but not why, so I asked him. His response was gentle but sure, I do not know why he responded I only know from God, that, that is exactly what I am meant to do."

From that moment on, my little girl began to recover to a large degree.

I could never have imagined for a moment that, that would be only one of many, many times when she would come close to death to the point of funeral arrangements being made and so on, and then she would suddenly snap back into life again.

She spent her first three weeks in a humidity crib unable to cry or utter a sound. I watched and waited day and night just for her to make some little sound, or make some small movement. Finally when she did she had such a strong male voice. She never cried with the sweetness of a little girl or a female then or for the rest of her life. Her voice was always deep, powerful and definitely a male voice.

That was the beginning of a time of her screaming almost day and night for close to three years. A blind man would have understood that type of crying and known that it came from serious pain. It broke my heart knowing I could never stop the pain or do anything of any real comfort for her except to hold her and cry along with her and did so on innumerable occasions.

As a young family we were not very welcome in many places because of the crying and screaming. However we did get to a few places which still hold fond memories for me. One such place was down by the beach, where she delighted in being held carefully in the shallow edges of the water, as the waves broke on the shore line, as she splashed furiously and actually laughed long and loud.

I would often place her on the dry sand just up from the edge of the water and she would bum scoot down to the water and splash her feet in it. She laughed at the wind as it blew directly into her face down by the beach. Another of the many things which she seemed to enjoy was the many trips of camping in the bush or in the mountains we went on as a family, with her younger brother and sister.

When she was approximately three months old and in the middle of an opera volume screaming time, I gently held her to me and said " Don't cry Tracey, Jesus will help you." The screaming instantly stopped and she stared in my face, with her mouth open. I was delightfully shocked and was more than willing to share such a wonderful though strange happening with another catholic couple of friends. I was instantly told that I had to be careful about speaking of such things because it was dangerous to do so and was not a real happening.

Unfortunately I listened to what I was told and did not repeat the happening for another five years.

For the first twelve months of her life, the medical staff loudly proclaimed that there was absolutely nothing wrong with her. Then suddenly they declared that she had a severe lack of mobility and that her chances of any normal life were not likely. Many other strange and untruthful conversations were held over the next five years.

I had witnessed many of her various fits and convulsions which left her limp and tired for the rest of the day. This happened many, many times over. Still at first, medics would not say there was actually anything wrong with her. The fits became so bad I recognised the danger of having her at home any longer because I was unable to protect or lift her during the seizures, especially out of the bath where most of her seizures were happening at that time. Home help or special care products for such illnesses were not available to me and many others in those times and I was no longer physically strong enough to fulfil her very real and constant needs.

She was placed in a government institution for the disabled, which at that time left me feeling like a traitor of a mother. I knew they were irrational thoughts but could never erase them from my guilt ridden brain for the rest of her time here on earth.

As parents we never got to do any of the normal things which most young parents were able to with their first baby. Never hearing her say as normal babies do mum or dad; that is except for one exceptional day when she was three months old, then never again afterwards. Never seeing her hold and play with any of the toys we bought her even before she was born. Never having the pleasure of seeing her take her first steps towards us. Then never seeing her walk as we held her hands.

Still there were some precious moments of very real treasures as I look back in retrospect.

Except for one day when she was three months old, travelling on a train to my brothers place in the country, where she held my thumb the whole way, she never did that or held any other finger till approximately six months before she died.

Each time when we would visit her in the government institution, it was so hard to try and communicate with her and I never knew if she actually recognised I was her mum or not on any of those visits. But I did have my heart broken afresh each time as she would begin to scream and scream as we left her ward to go home.

Over the following forty two years she did at different times say a couple of words when the medical staff was dealing with her in her every day care. She never held a full conversation with anyone or did any of the normal things normal children can do. She did however let you know she was not pleased when being held by the hand or even touched on the hand. She would either try kicking your legs or simply shove your hand away and on some occasions actually laugh as she did it, or scream at you.

Then one magic, beautiful day, after I turned my face directly towards her as I had said so many times previously "Gee Tracey, I really love you". She simply grabbed my thumb and held it for over ten minutes which reduced me to tears. That same day I recognised for the first time, what an incredible sense of humour she seemed to have had. My husband was sitting off to the side enjoying a good session of what I call arm chair politics. Tracey turned her? head towards him and laughed so loud that some of the staff came to see what the matter was. It was as if she knew what was being discussed and that it was really only guesses by folk who had no idea what they were talking about. As I said above, that was about six months before she died.

At the beginning of this annex I mentioned a treasure that was hard to give thanks for.

I am now compelled to share a treasure which cannot be denied or shut up any further. About thirty plus years ago I had become a spirit filled Christian and received the wonderful gift of speaking in tongues. Like I say, it was a gift of tongues not in any way a necessity to salvation. I truly valued this gift, which I also had received many years ago, because, I often ran out of my inadequate, English speaking words with my feeble efforts of giving all my cares and desires to our heavenly Father in the many areas of need in my life.

As I have also said, there were many times when my Tracey came close to death and then suddenly snapped back to life.

About one year before she finally died, she had become so ill she was admitted into hospital in critical care with possibly only two or three days to go.

Over the previous years I had slowly learnt to listen to the sweet, still but sure voice of our heavenly Father as he spoke to me in so many different ways. He spoke through the living word, through the preaching of many, through beautiful gospel music, through lessons in nature, through many dreams and visions and frequent conversations directly into my heart.

This was one of those times when he spoke directly into my heart. His words were "Anne, I am inviting you down to come and have fellowship with Tracey and me in hospital". I felt a little angry and felt definitely puzzled too. After all, how could this dying child of mine, who couldn't speak at all now, not even the few words she had managed over the previous years? So now how on earth was I supposed to have fellowship with her?

However, I felt urgency as He repeated the invitation several times, over the next day or two. I decided to go down and investigate what he may have meant.

I discussed it all with my husband, {Tracey's step dad} her biological father had died some years previously}.

I knew he is not really into all that sort of stuff, but I desired to submit by faith to his answer as I trusted our heavenly Father to speak through him. His immediate response was "I think we should go down there right now" We borrowed the money for fuel and headed off for the three hundred kilometre journey. When we got there it was obvious she didn't have long to go, she was unconscious, her organs were closing down and she had no longer any energy to move any muscles. She did not even flutter her eye lids. I tried everything possible to cause some kind of recognition or response and gave up in the end and cried aloud to my heavenly father, even though I was afraid to do such things in a public hospital.

His response in my heart was, just like the scripture; "Open your mouth and I will fill it." I then knew He meant open my mouth and begin to softly and simply pray in tongues. I was still afraid to do so because I did not want to get thrown out of my daughter's room only hours before she passed away. But the question continued to pose itself in my heart:

"Who was I going to please? Was I going to please man out of a fear of displeasing them and a fear of being rejected because of doing something strange which they did not understand; or was I going to step out in very bold faith and courageously obey what God was asking of me at the time?

I knew that I loved God enough to take the risk and so I did.

Instantly my daughter turned around from the waist up looked me right in the eyes and began to speak loudly and quite clearly in that same deep male voice, in another language. At that point I was still puzzled as to how we were actually supposed to converse with any sense. I felt The Father was saying that when I felt Tracey was asking a question I was to respond {still speaking in tongues} in an answering attitude. When I felt questions rising in my heart I was to speak with a questioning attitude. My husband recognised that it was an actual language even though he could not interpret the words. He became restless and went and spent time in the nearby shops which were close to the hospital. This conversation went on solidly for at least two hours and suddenly stopped. Tracey had the biggest male smile on her face as her lips became the shape and size of those of a thirtyish man. The smile seemed to freeze on her face so I thought she had just died. I sat there silently saying my goodbyes and felt that the smile had disappeared and only then did any staff re-enter the room where we were. The doctor was almost squealing with delight and couldn't stop asking Tracey, where she got the strange smile from, for she had never smiled like that before. I wondered how she would have responded if she had seen the first evidence of the smile on her face. Once more, Tracey snapped back into life only two days later.

We left there not long afterwards and drove home.

Of course I questioned our heavenly Father at length what it was all about. The first thing he reminded me of was though I had ached to know and perhaps even see Him smile at me, I never had; and that Tracey's smile was Him smiling at me through her. Then He reminded me, when the priest had given her the last rights six hours after she had been born, that she had been spirit filled at the same time, and had been speaking in tongues for the rest of her life. Because of His spirit being in her and I both, we had been able to communicate from spirit to spirit with each other at that crucial time of her life through the precious gift He had given us both. I had simply not recognised her gift from God all those years before;

Because, ashamedly I have to admit, I had never counted her able or good enough to have received such a precious gift.

If I had refused to go and have fellowship with Him and Tracey at that time, I would never have heard her speaking in tongues and been present at that special time of such miraculous fellowship.

I questioned why I never heard her before that and God lovingly showed me that I had arrogantly considered her as less than worthy to have received that precious gift. After all wasn't she only a disabled child? I was reminded that it is God alone who chooses who He gives

His lovely gifts to and who He considers as worthy or unworthy. After all, He looks on the heart and not on the outward appearance or limitations, as we do.

Then as if to seal that precious time of fellowship, in early April this year 2015 I had a phone call that once more she had been admitted into hospital and that she was deteriorating badly. Once more we borrowed the money and headed down there to see her and be with her just in case this was to be the last time.

We sat there for a while; she was again unconscious of course, with all her organs closed down and of course unmoving. After a short time they moved her into a more private room. Many of the staff from the government house where she had been living had come to say their good byes. Even the staff from the hospital had said their good byes to her. When they placed her in the private room, more staff from the community house where she had been living, came in to say good bye. I was becoming a little angry and jealous, waiting to be alone with her and my husband.

Then in walked a very tall African Negro. His head barely cleared the door frame. His face glowed so clearly I could barely see it. His mouth was definitely closed but I could hear him loudly singing and the music filled the room. Though I tried hard, I could no longer physically hold my mouth closed as I openly declared "Oh, so you are the one who is the singer aren't you."

He was amazed and I was in shock and feeling quite embarrassed. Then he explained he had never sung a note in public in his whole life, and asked how I knew he was a singer.

He said he had just joined the staff at the house but I knew I had never seen him there before. I told him he had been given a gift from God and now he was responsible to share it with the children which he loved so much. Only then did I see another woman standing at his side that spoke up and said that she was actually his boss. This woman had the exact same name as my daughter; Tracey. She turned to him and said, so now you have been told what to do so you had better do it. I do not believe I will ever see either of them again; unless in heaven.

As he walked over to Tracey's bed and barely touched the foot of the bed and said "Hellow Tracey how are you?" she gave a very distinct noise of greeting and opened her eyes enough of a slit to look at him, then turned and looked at me also. It was at that point I felt God say in my heart "Now sing to her" I began to sing ONE TWO THREE JESUS LOVES ME. Her eyes remained open though with just a slit till I finished, then she closed them for the last time, even though she did not actually pass on till a few hours later.

During the night my back became quite sore as I sat on the hard hospital chair that I had to go and lay down for a few hours about five o'clock the next morning. I was staying at my nieces place and so asked her right on ONE OCLOCK, late lunch time, if she had some chilli flakes or something similar for I was becoming icy cold. She gave me some lovely salmon casserole and I smothered it with the hot chilli flakes and still didn't taste it. A quarter of an hour later I received the phone call that Tracey had passed way at exactly one o'clock. I wanted to rush in straight away and see her, but was gently restrained by The Holy Spirit not to go for another hour and a half, which I obeyed.

On the way down to the hospital as we travelled from home to see her for the last time, as usual I had asked my heavenly Father if it pleased (H)im and if he saw fit, could I please hug Tracey one last time as she passed from this world to the next, because she had never been able to hug me through her life time.

I felt that He was asking me to release and surrender unto Him the last hug from Tracey, which I did do by faith even though it broke my heart to do so.

So now I thought, oh well, even though it hurt pretty badly I was not meant to be the last one to hold her as she died.

Finally the hour and half was up so we went in to see her for the last time and instinctively put my arm under her head and just sat there saying more silent goodbyes.

I felt once more the gentle but insistent prompting of my heavenly Father saying, open your mouth and say good bye. I was puzzled and argued a little about that; after all wasn't she already dead for an hour and forty minutes. Just do it, He responded.

The whole time I had my arm under her I could still feel the exact same level of body heat she had during the night before and I could clearly hear a strange but strong breathing near her mouth. I checked to make sure it wasn't either my husbands or my own breathing that I could hear and it definitely wasn't, in fact it was quite different.

I opened my mouth and said " Good bye my little angel" and instantly the body temperature dropped as it snapped cold as her spirit left her body and the breathing continued till a few more seconds as we stood up to leave.

So; what I had given to God in faith, Tracey's last hug, He had given back with much enlarged blessing and loving favour.

I believe it is a good thing to share a couple more strong points about this wonderful child of God. Many years ago my husband and I went to the large public institution where she had been for many years before she went into the community housing place. It was the Christmas break up for the whole institution. Much planning and care went into the preparations. It was strange weather. Cold one minute, raining the next then hot the next. The large marquees were assembled for each of the ward's. The food had been prepared and many decorations beautifully placed around the place. Many of the clients were under heavier than usual medication to keep them calm while visitors were around. They had become rather agitated perhaps because of the wild weather conditions. Some were actually asleep and strapped into their wheel chairs for their safety sake. Tracey was definitely one of the sleeping ones.

As the parent's and staff began to wheel the client's from the ward's to the marquees it began to rain heavily, thunder rolled and lightening flashed across the sky like angry serpents. The client's remained asleep but only till we reached the cover of the marquees.

The weather instantly became hot and stuffy, then cold and very windy. Then an incredible storm broke loose like a tormented lion breaking out of a lifelong cage. Cold wind blew people almost off their feet as it blew the heavy rain into the marquees. Within moments there was approximately three to four inches of water on the floor of each one of them. During the whole time that the rain was coming into the marquees and the ferocious storm lashed everything and everyone, Tracey stood erect on her feet, even though she remained strapped to the wheel chair. Her eyes opened larger than I had ever seen before, her face shone like a neon sign and she laughed so loud that many came to see what was happening. This went on for approximately forty minutes. The moment the storm ceased she fell asleep again and then dropped down again into her wheel chair. She always loved storms, just like I do, but this was the time most memorable where everyone had seen her pure delight at the display of God's Presence and Glory through weather conditions. I shall never forget the laughter and the glow on her face as it went on. She was truly like an eagle my little Storm Rider. Just like an eagle as it soars right up through the middle of a storm and then remains there till the storm is over.

I have to admit, Tracey never ever had a mean bone in her body regardless to whatever happened to her and in her during her whole lifetime. She was never ever nasty or grumpy and in fact she became quite the opposite. The older she got and the more pain she had as her seizures increased and other conditions became worse, the greater and more frequent she laughed, especially in the last four or five years of her life.

I have gone into some detail about the loss and life of my precious daughter, not just for self satisfaction or even an attempt to deal with grief though that is some small part of it. I have shared it openly, because I am fully aware that there are numerous mothers and fathers and loved ones who lose someone close to them and never share it with others because it is a truly too painful, personal thing to deal with. But still we all need to know and sometimes be reminded of the fact, God knows all about it in every detail. He has been there with you through every moment of pain, trouble, even torment at times and He counts the time you have gone through as highly valuable. Even though it may have appeared at times there was no real use or purpose for the one who had suffered so before they died. God has got a plan and a purpose for everyone He gives life to, regardless to the length of time spent here on earth. He counts them and every single one of us more precious than fine silver or gold.

I have also shared the story of my daughter's life, because I know beyond all shadow of doubt, there are most definitely very real and very rare treasures in every situation, every place and every person.

However, sometimes we need the tears and pain to make us look closer at what is happening and what is coming to the surface during our times of pain.

Of course we will all miss seeing many of those treasures but God does not give up on us or stop loving us and continues to place value and treasures everywhere we put our feet and mind. So I can now literally say with praise and thanksgiving "Father God, I thank and praise you for every single moment of my life, and every single moment of my precious daughter's life, though she suffered terribly every day she lived, every person who has come into contact with me and every situation I have gone through whether it has been painful, puzzling or joyful."

The greatest pearls are made through the greatest times of pain and suffering. Then they are brought into the light and seen and valued often beyond the normal man's ability to pay for them.

So what a privilege I have had, to be able to have had such a treasure of high price in my life. I now Praise God for all things at all times.

Except for the last ten years of her life when she had good care from the staff in the community housing;

There were many times while my daughter was in the government system that several illegal procedures' were done and much unacceptable medicinal trials were ministered to her. There were innumerable times over approximately thirty years of my seeking answers to serious questions, which were never answered. There were also many, many times when things were secretly done without my consent; I mention this because I was supposed to be her legal guardian; but that never had the expected respect or honour to which it was due.

Over the years I had seriously considered to take my story to the media, not only for my own satisfaction and help but to let the public know at least some of what was happening to many of our vulnerable children in government institutions.

However, the actual moment when my daughters spirit left her body God took the total anger and anguish of the previous forty eight years out of my heart. He totally took from my heart the need to have it all published and for me to seek legal satisfaction. I knew then He had taken control of all the unanswered things and illegal happenings and would be dealing with all of it in His own perfect timing and in His own way, but for His glory and not just for my personal satisfaction, and not even just for the protection of all the other people who had gone through such places.

He took the pain also that goes with such a devastating time from the previous years.

I could never have accepted such a calm and forgiving attitude if anyone else had shared it with me about their loss and frustrations. And yes, I have forgiven all that has happened to my daughter and me. But after experiencing such a miraculous and immeasurable blessing for myself, I can now share that fact with as many who wish to hear it, and be truthful and at peace with joy about it at the same time as I praise and thank God for the whole journey of my life and that of my daughter.

Without Tracey as a very real part of my life I would most definitely have missed seeing many of the treasures with which I was privileged to and gathering many of them. Sometimes we all need to be stopped, or at least slowed down, to see what lays at our feet as our own special treasures before we stumble over them. When we have stumbled over many treasures we have then frequently complained and become angry and so forth and often turned away from God.

But still, He never gives up on loving us or bringing treasures into our life, so that we can grow by them and enjoy seeing His wonderful care as He continually adds unto us life and that more abundantly.

INDEX FOR SCRIPTURE REFERENCES ALL REFERENCES FROM KING JAMES BIBLE EXCEPT REFERENCE 51

This comes from The Amplified Version of the bible.

Ref {29} Luke 10 :25-37

Ref {30} Isaiah 40 :1

Ref {31} Psalm 91:4

Ref {32} Romans 8: 28

Ref {33} Philippians 4:4

Ref {34} Psalm 136: 1

Ref {35} John 15:1-9

Ref {36} 1 Kings 19:12

Ref {37} Deut.33:27

Ref {38} John 14:1

Ref {39} Philippians 4:6

Ref {40} Matthew 28:20

Ref {41} Romans 8:31-39

Ref {42} Isaiah 55:8

Ref {43} Deut.31:6

Ref {44} Philippians 4:19

Ref {45} Hebrews 10:24

Ref {46} Isaiah 55:8

Ref {47} Ephesians 4:16

Ref {48} Deut.33:27

Ref {49} Matthew 25:45

Ref {50} Romans 4:17

Ref {51} Ephesians 3:20

Ref {52} Deut.33:27

Ref {53} Luke 21:15+Exodus 4:12+Ezekial 3:27+Matthew 10:19

Ref {54} Psalm 81:10

Ref {55} Deut.31:6

Ref {56} I John 4:18

Ref {57} Psalm 18:30

Ref {58} Ephesians 2:6

Ref {59} I Samuel 16:7

Ref {60} John 6:36

Ref {61} Proverbs 3:6

Ref {62} I Corinthians 10:13

Ref {63} Ecclesiastes 3:1

Ref {64} John 15:1

Ref {65} Hebrews 4:13

Ref {66} 1 Corinthians 10:13+Ecclestiases 3:1

Ref {67} Romans 8:1

Ref {68} John 7:38

Ref {69} Revelations 22:1

Ref {70} 1 Corinthians 2:9

Ref {71} Philippians 4:6-7

Printed in the United States
By Bookmasters